THE MULTIPLE LIVES
OF A BLANK BOOK

Published by Booksfromthefuture as part of
Booksfromthefuture Summer School 2015,
a ten-day workshop on transdisciplinary
inquiry and publishing led by Yvan Martinez
and Joshua Trees with Krister Olsson at
London Centre for Book Arts.

John Freeman, Gustavo Grandal Montero,
Federico Antonini and Esa Matinvesi
provided invaluable perspectives and
feedback throughout the process.

Published in parallel with *But now space was
part of the object*[1] by Masaki Miwa and
Ying Tong Tan (Booksfromthefuture and
Zyxt, 2015).

Edited by Yvan Martinez and Joshua Trees
with Krister Olsson

Designed by Joana Chicau, Cecilia Denti,
Matheus de Paula, Luana Graciano,
Claude Marzotto, Yvan Martinez,
Kevin McCaughey, Krister Olsson,
GaEun Ryu, Joshua Trees, Lena Wurz

Typeset in Univers Else by OSP
(Open Souce Publishing)

Special thanks to London Centre for Book
Arts, Special Collections at Chelsea College
of Arts Library and Makoto Yamada

Printed by Lulu

booksfromthefuture.info

ISBN 978-0-9573509-3-9

MLBB053

978 0 957350939

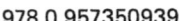

THE MULTIPLE LIVES
OF A BLANK BOOK

BOOKSFROMTHE-
FUTURE

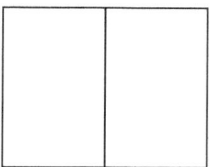

7   Yvan Martinez
        Joshua Trees
        Krister Olsson
9   Federico Antonini
23   John Freeman

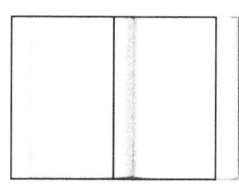

27   Joseph Townshend
33   Kristian Henson
39   Niko Mihaljevic
45   Per Törnberg
49   Lena Wurz
55   Luana Graciano
57   Seiko Watanabe
63   Simon Goode
        Ira Yonemura

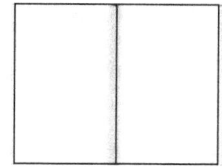

67   Esa Matinvesi
69   Hirofumi Isoya
71   Spassky Fischer
73   Hyunho Choi
77   Jangs Müller
85   Tomoko Kawai
87   Cecilia Denti
89   Jen Lee
95   Kevin McCaughey
97   Corbin Mahieu
99   Jozef Ondrik
103   Helge Hjorth
        Bentsen
105   Makoto Yamada
109   Sean Kuhnke
121   Pimeriko
125   GaEun Ryu
127   Joana Chicau

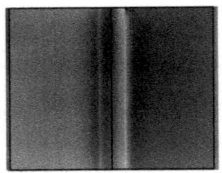

137	Ayse Koklu
141	Clara Lobregat Balaguer
151	Kasper Pyndt
167	Matheus de Paula
169	Marie Lécrivain
173	Masaki Miwa
181	Rita Matos
185	Luigi Amato

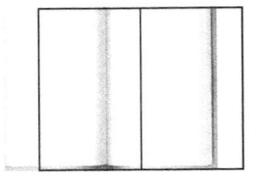

242	Thomas Hervé
246	Ying Tong Tan
250	Claude Marzotto
256	David Horvitz
262	Rafaela Drazic
264	Risa Tsunegi
266	River Jukes-Hudson
274	Ryo Shimizu
284	Darius Ou Dahao

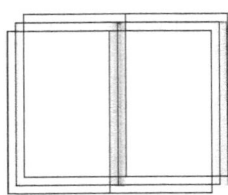

227	Eric Hu
229	Ghazaal Vojdani
233	Jan Novák
235	Neil Donnelly
237	Nobuo Yoda
239	Soji Shimizu

Historically, the *bookness* of the book has been defined primarily in terms of its material, structural and technological qualities. Philip Smith claims to have coined the term, though Richard Minsky remembers things a bit differently – Google them to witness an interesting feud. Ulises Carrión, Paul Chan, Johanna Drucker, Clive Phillpot and Thomas Vogler have all offered definitions that encompass broader variables of *bookness* – aesthetic, cultural, metaphysical, psychological, phenomenological, symbolic, etc. This has encouraged us to conduct our own practice-based research with the aim of learning about and contributing to the constantly changing meaning of *bookness*.

The multiple lives of a blank book started as a conversation between ourselves and Krister Olsson about the Web as an imperfect and influential research environment and the potential for publishing to function as a *cultural algorithm* between the Web and contemporary life. We discussed how books have become performative objects that get encountered and experienced in multiple contexts simultaneously, and increasingly through documentation in the mirror universe of the Web.

We were particularly intrigued by Die Antwoord's adoption of the terms *documentary fiction* and *hyperreality* to describe themselves and their artistic practice in response to their *authenticity* being questioned, as well as by Spencer McCall's documentary film *The Institute* which reconstructs the story of an alternate reality game created by Jeff Hull that ultimately engaged over ten thousand participants in

an act of collective artifice.

Eventually we agreed upon the idea of sending copies of a blank book to fifty contributors accompanied by an invitation to partake in a game of *documentary fiction*.[1] Contributors were prompted with an open-ended suggestion to use the provided book as an object, symbol, tool or prop for conducting and documenting experimental enactments of the worlds that such a book might inhabit and inspire. Blankness – or bareness – seemed like the best way to strip the book of pre-existing meaning, aside from the inescapable connotations of being a book.

The documentation collected has been curated and presented as a sequence of deeds, episodes, tableaus and vignettes that seeks to reveal as much about the people and places involved as it does about the book. This story would not have been possible if not for the contributors who generously agreed to play along.

Yvan Martinez and Joshua Trees
with Krister Olsson
London, September 2015

1 [...] *One general assumption is that these works emerge from the interstice of documentary and fiction – but what other boundaries do they operate between? Observation and instigation, life and art, the actual and possible, translation and interpretation, presence and performance, construction and deconstruction, evidence and hearsay, authorship and plagiarism, meaning and abstraction.* Luke Moody, *Act normal: hybrid tendencies in documentary film*, 2013.

GUY MONTAG

Around twenty minutes into François Truffaut's
Fahrenheit 451, fireman Guy Montag flips through
the pages of a blank paperback book dug out of one
of those thermos bottles used for keeping beverages
warm. The gesture, executed with an expression of
conceit and disenchantment, reveals a wavering faith
in a society based on the censorship of knowledge,
invention and interpersonal relationships through
the systematic destruction of its most efficient
vehicle: the book. The paper book. This movement,
much like the extraction of a rabbit from a magi-
cian's hat, is the pinnacle of a brief demonstration
that the protagonist offers to some young firemen
at the Fahrenheit 451 fire station, during which he
illustrates a few of the possible techniques employed
by the rebels in order to hide and circulate the
books that escaped the great blazes of the book
burning carried out by the dictatorship.

The brief sequence, which appears exclusively in
the cinematic version, in Jean Louis Richard's
and François Truffaut's adaptation, but not in
Ray Bradbury's book, displays a set of visual and
symbolic elements which turn this simple prop into
a significative instance that helps to introduce some
atypical publishing acts, linked to one another by
the lack of information of any nature impressed
upon the surface of their pages.

To blank out the pages of the demonstrative book is
the only way the military body has at their disposal
to show cadets what a book looks like without

showing them an actual printed book. The fact that the firemen themselves cannot use printed book copies to show the citizens of the book-burning dictatorship what a book looks like, is symptomatic of the psychological terrorism and of the suspicion strategy at the core of the dystopian society described in *Fahrenheit 451*; in retaliation, the (maliciously) monotheistic prohibition of depiction results in producing exactly the opposite effect, bestowing meaning and a mysterious aura to the book extracted from the thermos, transforming it from *no book* to *all books*.

But the element which is charged with a bookish symbology beyond any other is the fact that, according to the protocol of the cadets' lesson, it is the book with limited dimensions and with a soft cover that is considered the most dangerous one for the regime – the paperback – synonymous with the democracy and mass distribution that marked the 20th century. The soft cover and reduced dimensions that lowered production costs are regarded by the dictatorship as facilitators and accomplices of the underground and of the surreptitious; unlike large leather-bound volumes, these objects can be hidden within other objects or containers, the shapes of which do not give away the hidden volume.

PLACING THE BLANK BOOK

The expression *artist's book* is often used to describe, without particular distinction, a wide variety of artifacts, each one characterized by different intentions, executing methods, provenance

and distribution – artifacts that in this respect are indeed sometimes diametrically opposite – setting indiscriminately side by side Ed Ruscha and Picasso, Dieter Roth and William Morris. The variety of different publications within this indistinct magma include altered books in unique editions, three-dimensional artworks that encompass books, limited edition *sculpture books*, pop-up books, flip-books, limited edition classics printed and bound with luxury materials, limited edition exhibition catalogues, graphic designers' books, typographers' books, prints and graphic works by artists bound in the form of books and accompanied by essays or by comments taken from literature classics, artists' projects conceived in the form of books in extensive editions as well as different possible combinations of the above.

Regardless of the first examples of this lateral and meta-narrative concept of a book, such as in Sterne, Mallarmé, Blake and others, the expansion and diffusion as well as the consequent loss of its consideration as a mute container of linear text has been a characteristic phenomenon of the 20th century and it could have never occurred in a time in history different than the one that bore witness to the birth of the paperback, a book affordable to everyone.

The need to trace precise limits is the result of a copious art production in the form of printed publications related to the conceptual art of the Sixties in the USA and of the critical and curatorial assimilation that began retrospectively in the following decade with *Book as artwork* (Celant, 1971),

Six years (Lippard, 1973) and *Artists books* (Perrault, 1974). The books, magazines and *ephemera* included in these collections, in tune with the context that generated them, demonstrate the special attention conceptual artists (and others alike) pay to the book as a specific medium and how they refuse to consider it a stack of bound luxury multiples or as the documentation of an exhibition; *Six years* is a collection of material of radically different origins where the only linearity taken into consideration is the chronologic one, as though it were a verbal-visual diary.

The most specific definition, an intersection between looking inside a microscope and a declaration of love to the book as a medium, appears in the late Sixties, in the form of a long distance dialogue, in the writings and conferences between Clive Phillpot, a librarian at MoMA from 1977 and Ulises Carrión, a Mexican artist relocated to Amsterdam. The former had to confront some obvious and complex sets of problems, since the material that was to be archived came in shapes and formats of a particularly heterogeneous nature. An emblematic case is that of *A portfolio of piles*, by the N.E. Thing Co. collective: a collection of sheets that look like postcards. How is such an object to be catalogued? As a book? As an artist multiple? Making things all the more complicated was the artists' initial intention of making their publications available even *on the shelves near the check-out counters in supermarkets* (Lippard, 1973) as well as the conservation criteria set up by librarians, in complete antithesis to the art market that was investing in and re-evaluating even relatively poor and utilitarian editions. Ruscha for example

signed his first edition of *Twentysix gasoline stations*, enormously increasing the value of an object initially sold for about two dollars. How is a paperback book supposed to be archived, if it is also destined to become a collectible cult object?

Ulises Carrión, who had begun his career as a writer and poet and who had published two novels, *La muerte de Miss O* (1966) and *De Alemania* (1970), began devoting himself to the visual arts in the early Seventies. But his approach was deep-seated in his previous production. His vision of art, art criticism and art market formed his systematic opinions in this regard, which he expressed in his essays and manifestos, situated somewhere between the specificity of a modernist medium in *The new art of making books* (1975) and the pervading refusal of the commercialization of the speculative thought that emerges in his essay *Critical autonomy of the artist* (1979). Carrión exemplifies the knocking down of barriers between artistic practice and everyday life and the bookshop he opened in Amsterdam in 1975, that dealt with art publishing – Other Books and So – faithfully reflects this. He principally dealt with limited editions of what at a later stage he would define as *bookworks*, printed with modest means such as the mimeograph, in order to keep production and selling costs low while facilitating their dissemination.

Both the term *bookwork* – within which blank books could probably be included too – and its definition are hard to delineate chronologically. Clive Phillpot drew up a chronology in the short text

Traversing the field of artists' books for the catalog of *Fahrenheit 39* art book fair 2014 in Italy.

In 1973, in a column in *Studio International*, Phillpot uses the term *book art* when referring to Celant's selection of books in 1971. His intention was to align it to terms such as *land art*, *video art*, *mail art*, *body art*, though he was aware of the resemblance of the formula with *art of books*, which indicated a book production that entailed hand-made processes and luxury materials, in other words the very antithesis of that which he was trying to pinpoint and define.

In 1974 the British Council's itinerant exhibition entitled *Artist's bookworks* included artist's books that curator Martin Attwood defined as works of art in the shape of a book with the maximum output between democratic diffusion and production costs.

In 1976, the year prior to his appointment as a librarian at the MoMA, Phillpot writes, in the *Artists' books* exhibition catalog:

> *Work falling into the category of book art can be defined as books in which the book form is intrinsic to the work.* (Phillpot, 2012)

That which was defined as a medium by Celant, Phillpot hastily defines as a constitutive and intrinsic shape and value of the artwork. The key moment comes somewhere around 1980 with the presentation of Ulises Carrión's text *Bookworks revisited*, that contains the aforementioned description by

Phillpot where the term *book art* is substituted by *bookwork*, a term borrowed from the title of an exhibition curated by Barbara London in 1977. Moreover, according to Carrión, *bookwork* contains no references to the craft of the author, shifting the attention to the book itself, and making the provenance and principal activity of the person producing it a secondary matter. Keeping in mind his other writings, this affirmation sounds like a proposal for a blend of underground primitivism and Greenberg's medium specificity.

In *Artforum* in 1982 Phillpot points out that the quote from his text is incorrect, nevertheless he willingly accepts it and will go on using it for many years.

In *Quant aux livres/On books*, a retrospective collection of essays, Anne Mœglin-Delcroix introduces a selection of Carrión's writings, in which, with the maturity obtained in the twenty years that followed the *Bookworks revisted* presentation and with the acknowledgement of the failure of the proposed nomenclature admitted by Phillpot himself (Phillpot, 2012), she gives credit to both Phillpot's and Carrión's writings as being the first sparks of real criticism in a field that lacked theorizing up to that moment; but she prefers to speak of specificity and of reciprocal expression and enhancement between verbal-visual information and the specific physical characteristics of the book, distancing herself from the subset diagram that today could appear much like a well-written quibble.

In referring to Dieter Roth's books, Johanna Drucker claims that no other medium exists for translating them and for incarnating the ideas upon which they

stand (Drucker, 2004).

Not all those concerned have considered the microscope as the most suitable tool through which to study the problem:

> *Critics, dealing with a relatively new medium, have generated the question of its boundaries, dividing the book into different typologies, each one functional to the different executive modalities. This eventually caused them to lose sight of the subversive capacity of an object that, though with great effort, is recognised as an essential guide for the comprehension of the artistic events of the century* [...].

> *And once again Celant's title comes as an aid. Therefore, books that maintain the shape and structure of the book but which, through the sovereignty of the artist's intentions are works of art.* (Maffei, 2006)

Maffei's vision is milder and focuses on the question of the artist and his point of view, setting himself in an antithetical position both to Carrión and Phillpot.

What is perplexing is the poor impact that this debate has had on the history of book design and communication, as though the microscopical analysis carried out in order to highlight the *intrinsic* nature of the book as a functional and irreplaceable element had been merely an obsessive and sterile cataloguing of a zealous librarian. As a matter of fact, the definition of *bookwork* is closely affiliated to design and to the field of publishing; the

incitement to consider the book medium as a system
of rules generated through a series of structural
and systemic restrictions (Kraus, 2005) cannot be
indifferent to book designers, graphic designers
and editors, especially in relation to the prophecies
on the death of the book, announced on various
occasions throughout the Sixties. To consider a
remediation (according to the term coined by
Jay David Bolter and Richard Grusin to define the
media that reproduce other media) of a *bookwork*
in a digital format, is impossible if one does not
admit the specific values of the new medium;
consequently the interdependence between a *book
specific* narrative and a book as active frame could
be considered a characteristic inherent to its identity
and thus irreplaceable by an electronic format.

How is all this related to blank books? The answer
may seem somewhat tautological. If the books
described by Clive Phillpot and introduced by Ulises
Carrión are nothing but a restricted niche within
an already ample context, could the *implausible
fertility* of blank books (Luthi, 2010) be inserted in
that narrow Boolean intersection? The concept is
simultaneously the vehicle. Furthermore, the narrative transmitted in a blank book can be used (read,
looked at, perceived) exclusively through the blank
book, making the division between paratext, material constitution and symbolic aura impossible. The
presence of the book appears absolutely *intrinsic*
and hardly re-mediable through other solutions.

Having taken note of the lack of an exhaustive
treatise in the writings of those who have dealt

with similar arguments, like Richard Kostelanetz, Cornelia Lauf, Johanna Drucker, and Clive Phillpot, I proposed this argument to them. All perspectives were concordant with mine, except Phillpot's; notwithstanding Carrión's affirmation:

The most beautiful and perfect book in the world is a book with only blank pages, in the same way that the most complete language is that which lies beyond all that the words of a man can say.

Every book of the new art is searching after that book of absolute whiteness, in the same way that every poem searches for silence. (Carrión, 1975)

Even though Phillpot states that *Dieter Roth in Greenland* is one of his favourite artist's books, he considers blank books as *book objects* and as chiefly sculptural works, where symbolism and the physicality of the object are primary factors with respect to the fruition and the reinvention of the sequence, a concept also dear to Carrión:

A book is a sequence of spaces. Each of these spaces is perceived at a different moment – a book is also a sequence of moments. (ibid.)

This very concept is also present in other examples, such as *Universum* and *Lost for words*, but in some cases thanks to the context (*Tabula rasa*) or interaction (*Sounds*) these could be considered *bookworks*, especially when keeping Carrión's words in mind:

In order to read the old art, knowing the alphabet is

enough. In order to read the new art one must appre-hend the book as a structure, identifying its elements and understanding their function. [...]

There are fast-reading methods because writing methods are too slow. To read a book, is to perceive sequentially its structure.

The old art takes no heed of reading. The new art cre-ates specific reading conditions. (ibid.)

It is the act of reading that should be reassessed and probably also renamed and brought closer to a wider concept of experience and interaction. Many blank books, rather than demanding to be perceived as sculptural and symbolic entities, urge the reader to find a new way of interacting with their pages.

The re-evaluation of the act of reading in its spatio-temporal conception can be explained and enriched through the words Matthew Kirschenbaum, associate Professor of English literature at Maryland University, wrote for *I read where I am*, a collection of essays curated by Mieke Gerritzen, Geert Lovink and Minke Kampman in 2011:

Reading is an event, not an act. Books are incidental (in the fullest meaning of the word). Texts are signals, transmissions. This is where I am now when I read, not a place but a mode, not a favourite chair but a state and frame. Think of it as resolution. (Gerritzen, Lovink, Kampman, 2011)

Phillpot's and Carrión's viewpoints also differ in

their way of considering the books of Ruscha, Weiner and Dieter Roth: regardless of the breach they brought about in the old conception of the book, they are defined as *non naïf* (Carrión, 1980), as if they had understood the intimate and specific potential of the book, but refused to accept the *new art's* economic and social consequences. Weiner was affiliated with Seth Siegelaub's gallery, a relationship on which he managed to capitalize, making conceptual art saleable to collectors, a development incompatible with Carrión's manifestos. Carrión even wrote that any comic book or a page taken from any newspaper proposes far more stimulating and complex reading methods than any conceptual art book, referring in particular to the Art & Language group (ibid.).

The blank book Carrión speaks of is not so much a concrete proposal, but rather a mirage, the hope of a book *to come*, conceived and realized in a lateral way, far from the official art circuits. Carrión himself produced no blank book at all and in fact such a publication would have been out of context with the rest of his productions and writings, which, regardless of the rigid communicative forms used, such as programmatic manifestos, never become dogmatic and are always open to interpretation. In *The new art of making books*, right after the part dedicated to the blank book, we read: *Intention is the mother of rhetoric*.

This text is an excerpt from the forthcoming publication *Blank Books Revisited*, (Nero, 2016), originally written as a postgraduate research thesis by Federico Antonini and supervised by Leonardo Sonnoli at ISIA in Urbino, Italy.

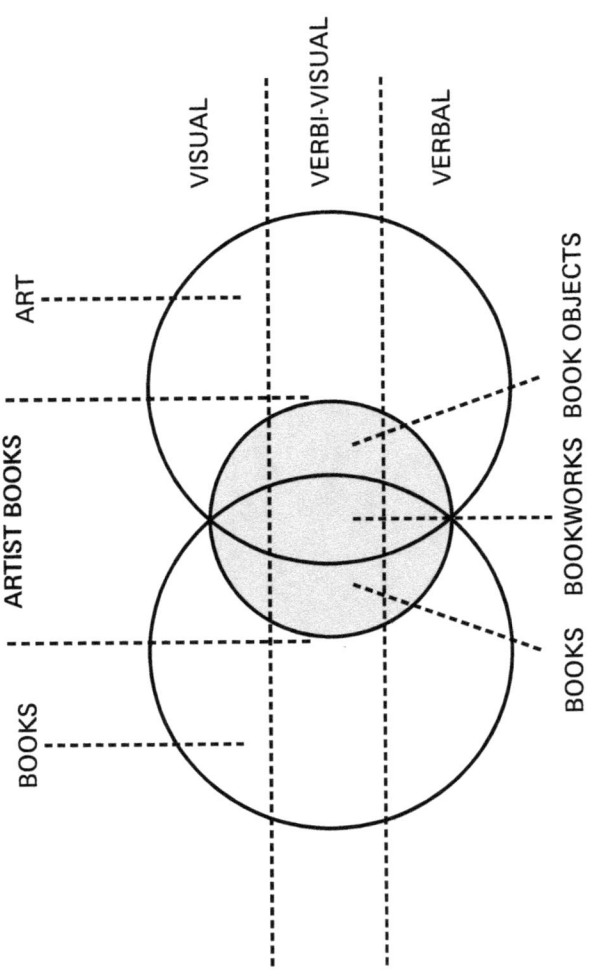

VISUAL

VERBI-VISUAL

VERBAL

ART

BOOK OBJECTS

ARTIST BOOKS

BOOKS   BOOKWORKS

BOOKS

Recreation of Clive Phillpot's diagram from *Outside of a dog*, 2003

LEAVE THE LIGHT ON

News of a recall,
Derivatives say it's no
Longer cheaper to settle,
The death vector climbing
Upward, trucks packed
Like bunk beds ferrying
Broken throttled vans
north across
Salt crusted planes, you
Said to always follow
The left margin, avoid
Hypnosis, the speedometer
a steady 72,
The state trooper explained
Ten or less and you're
Fine. So mirror, side mirror
Ahead, snow falling,
Fields of wheat sleep
Beneath winter's white
Coat, look at the nails
To gauge health, take
A break for safety's
sake, there is no
Such thing as a safe
Smoke. Count the miles
Until your exit. We'll
Leave a light on.

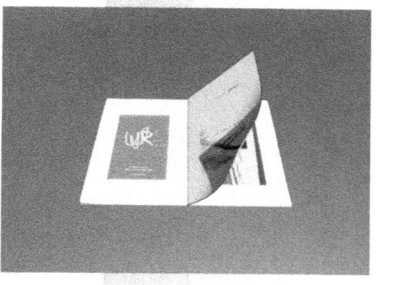
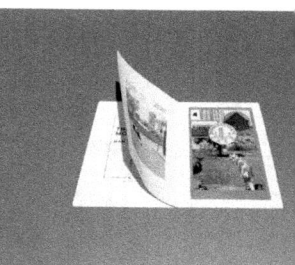
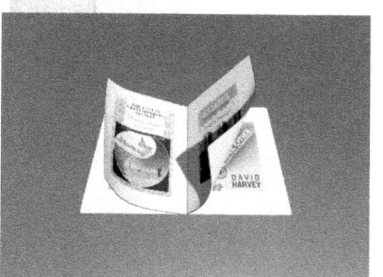
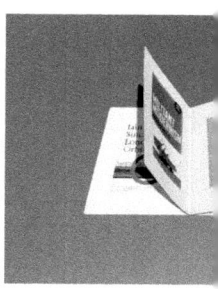

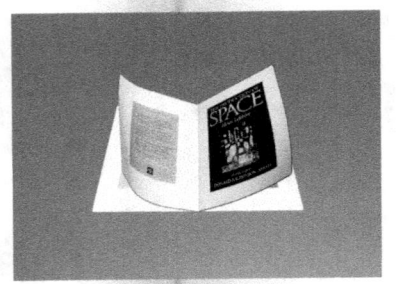 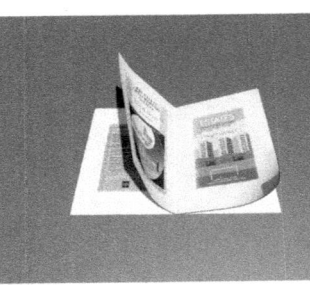

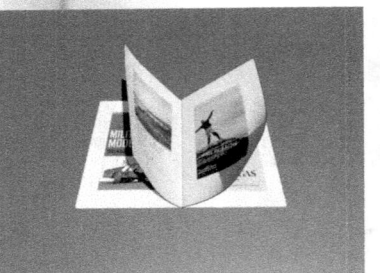 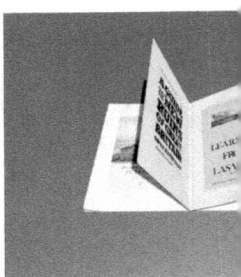

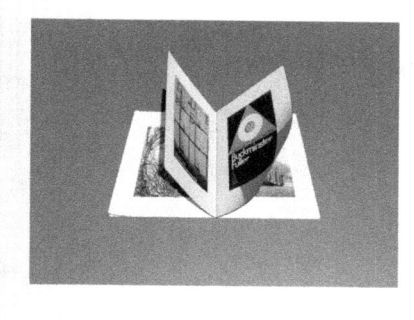

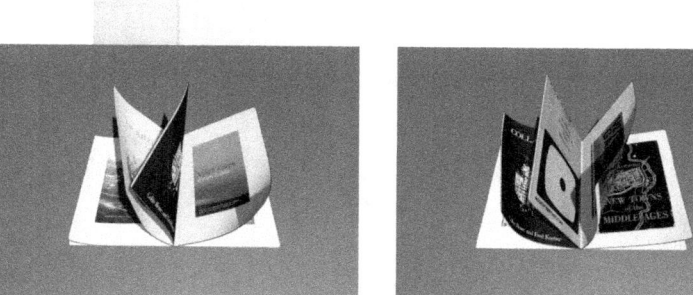

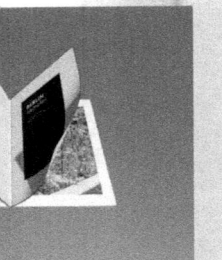

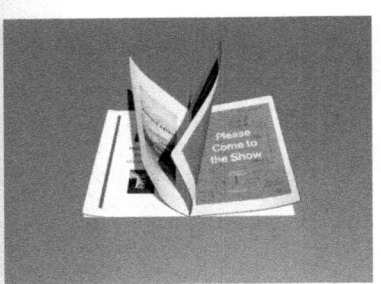

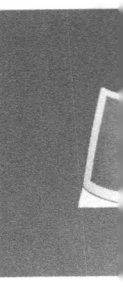

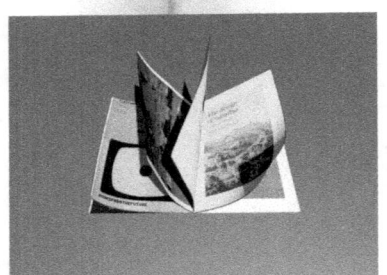

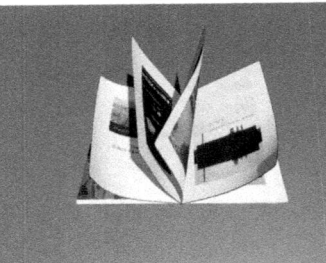

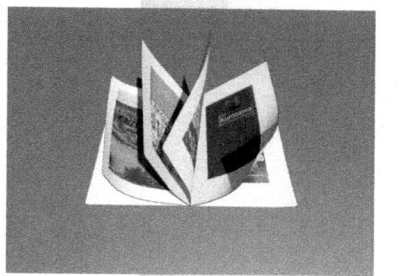 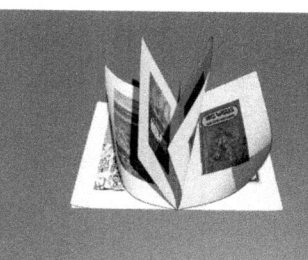

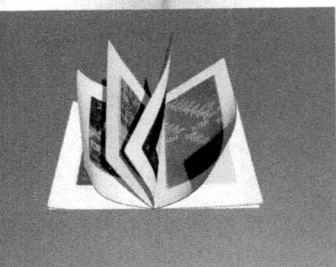

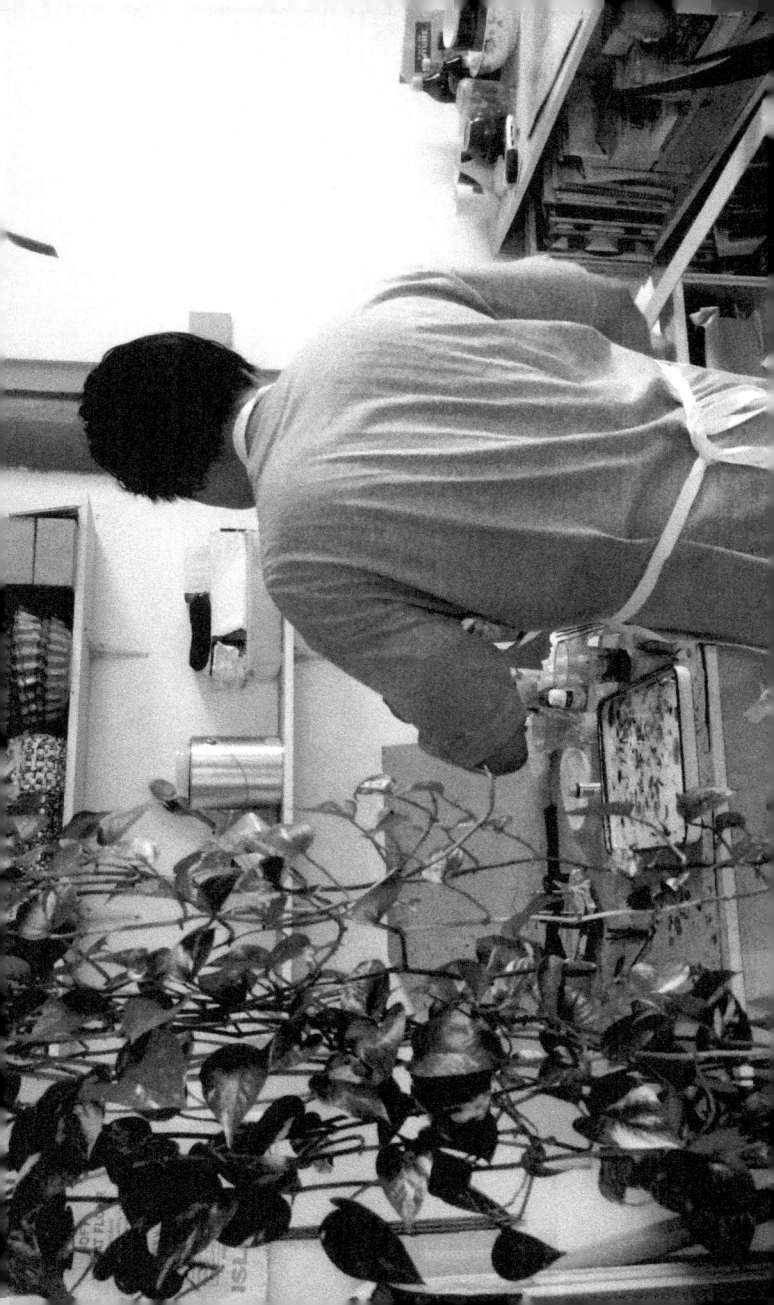

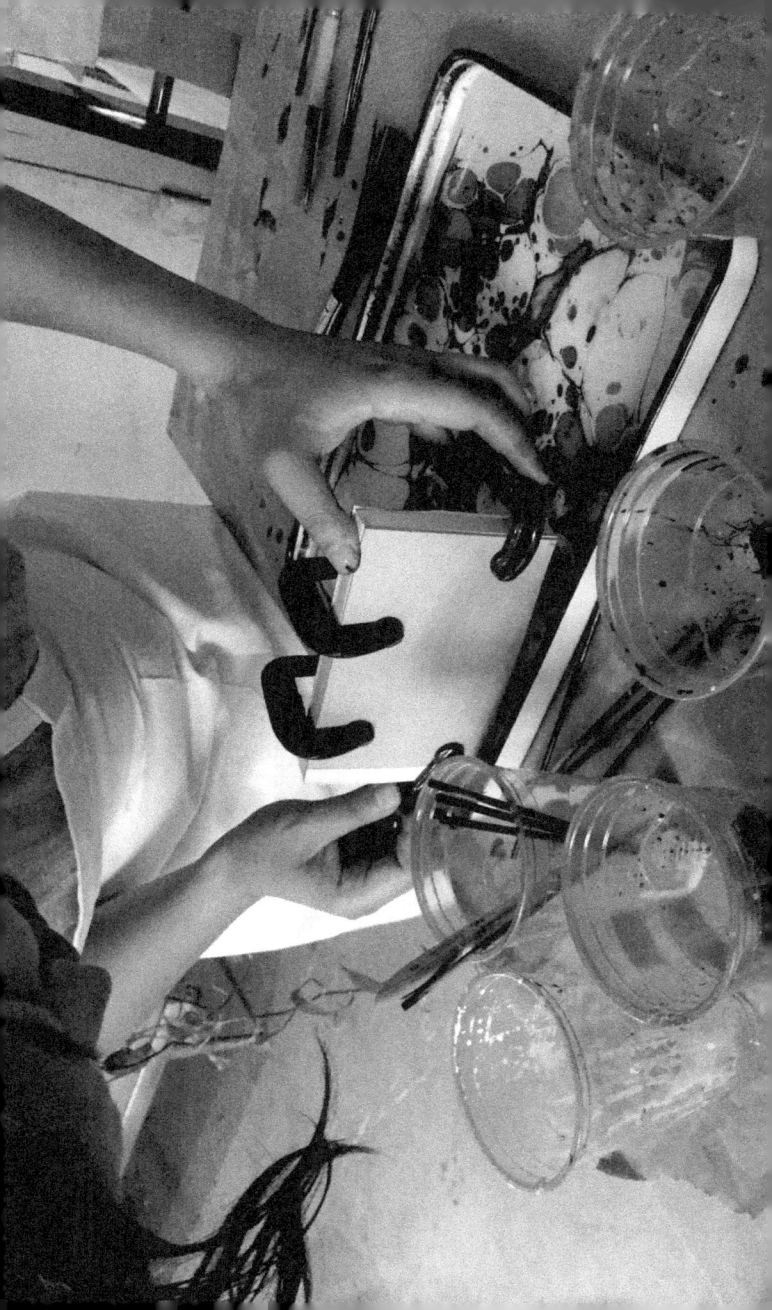

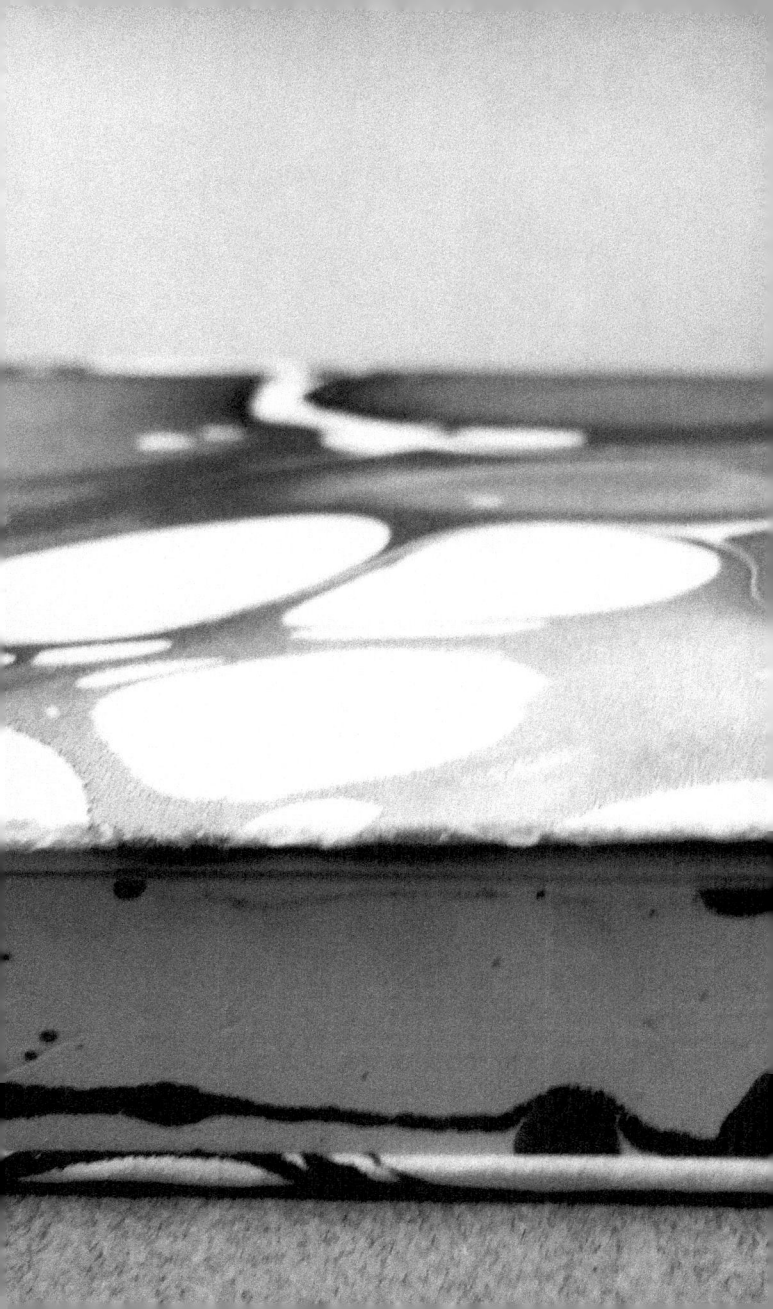

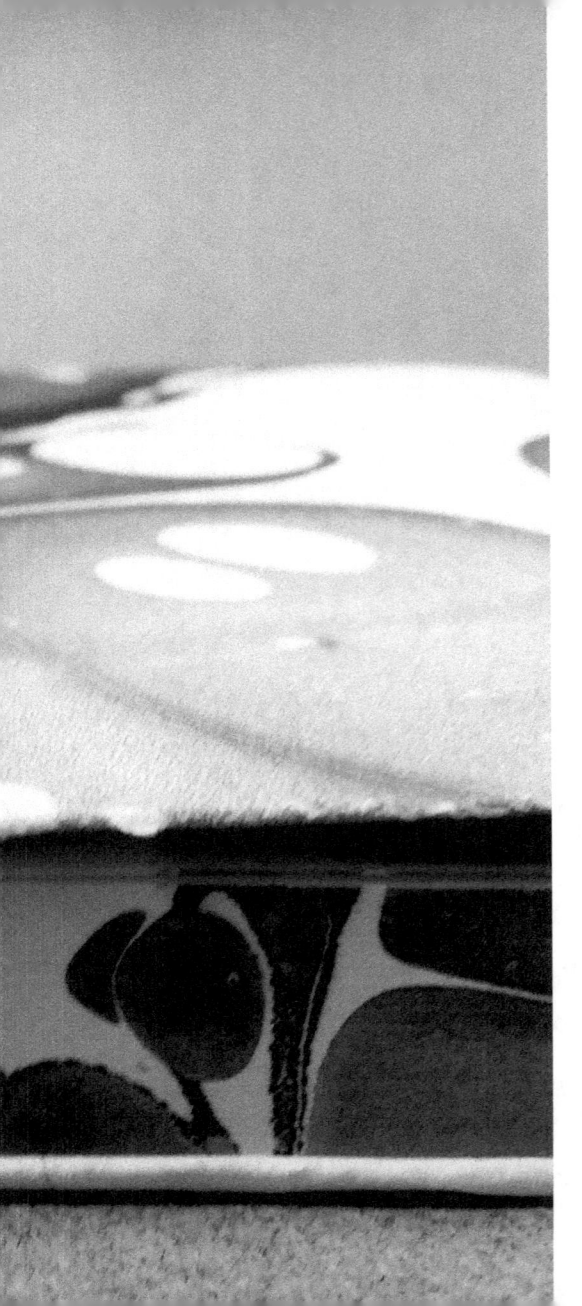

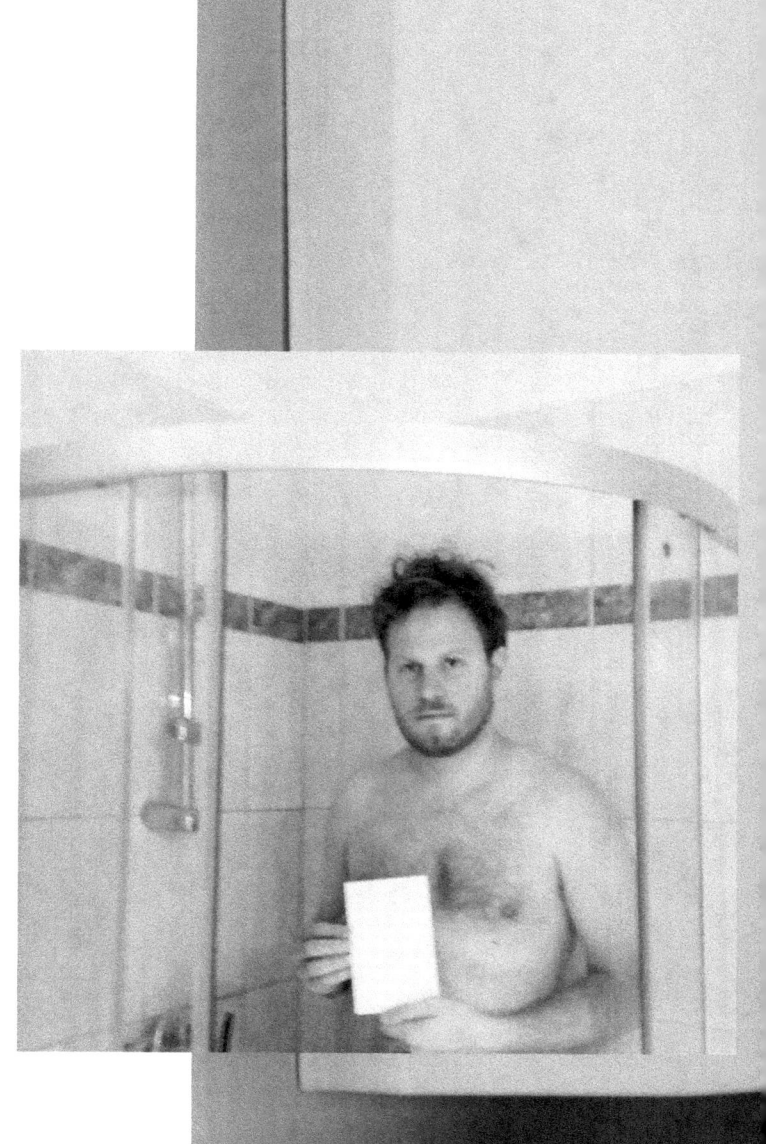

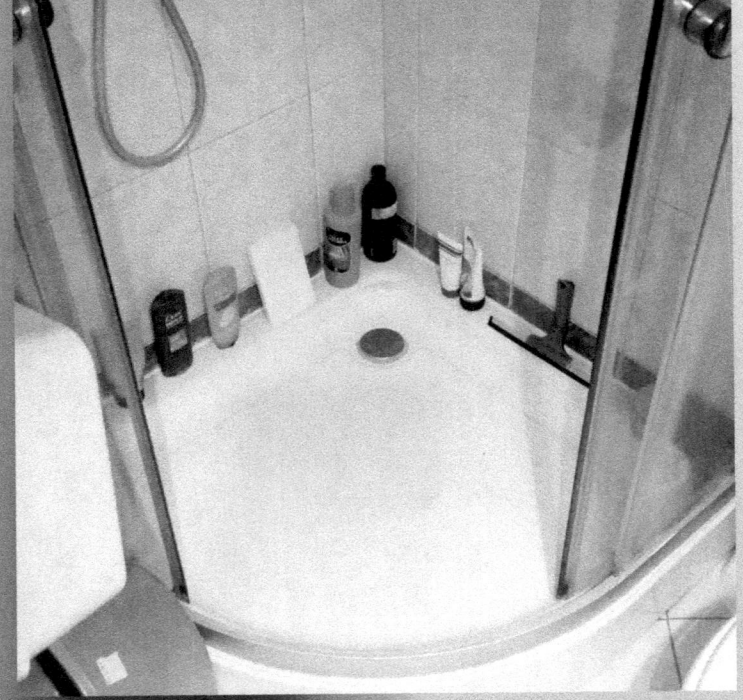

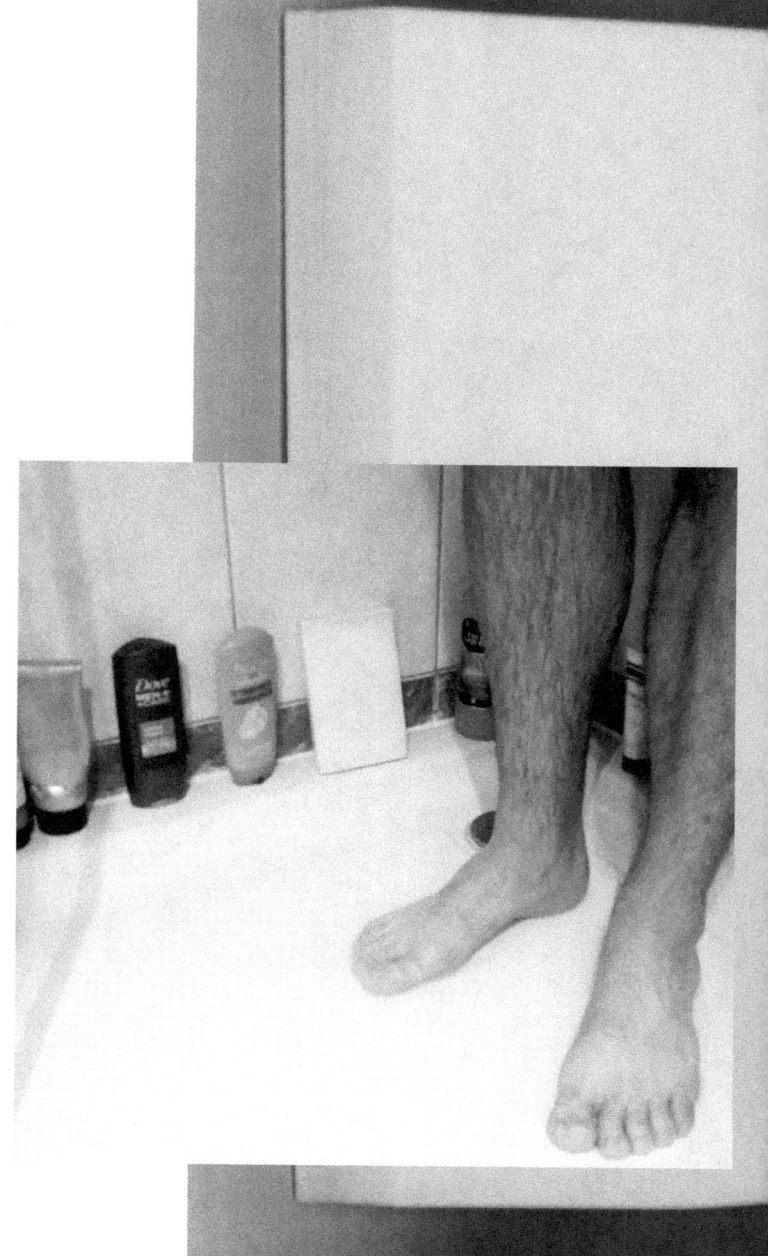

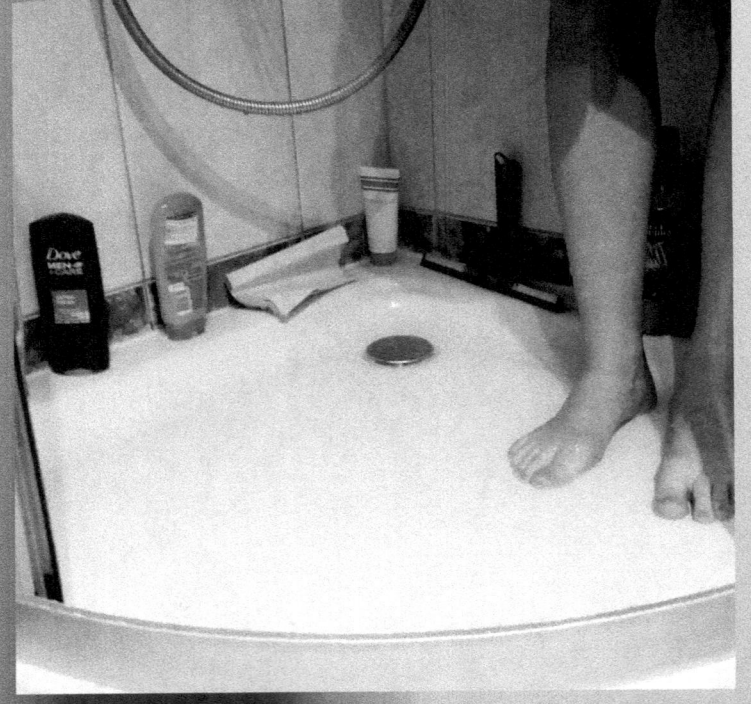

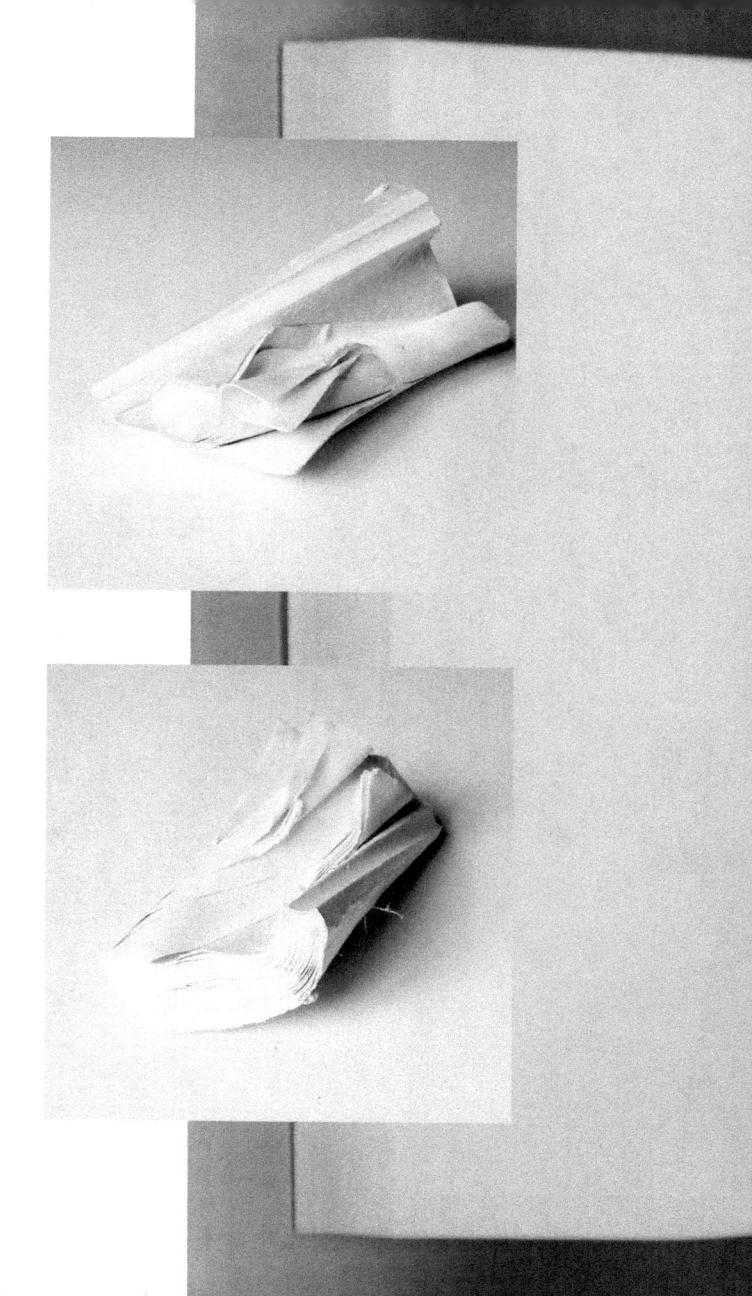

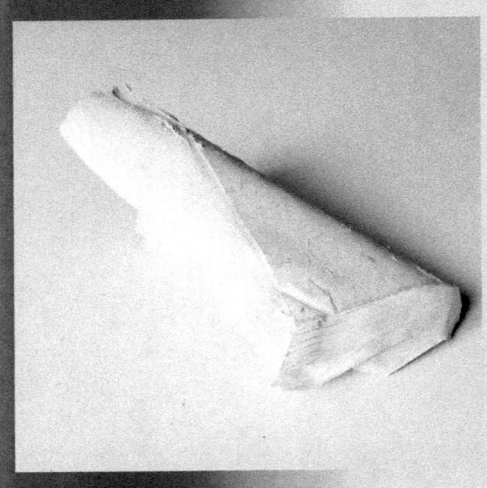

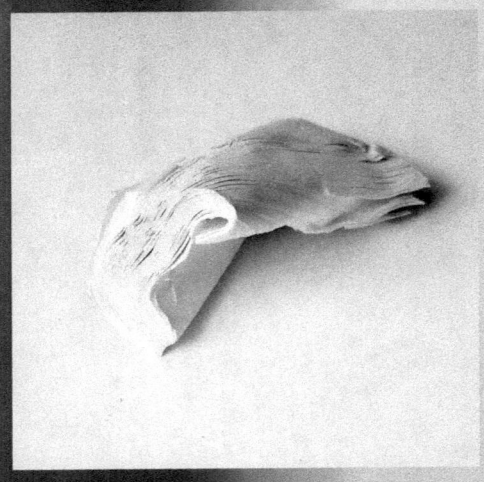

JILL SPENCER
MICROWAVE COOKBOOK

The complete guide to a new way of cooking

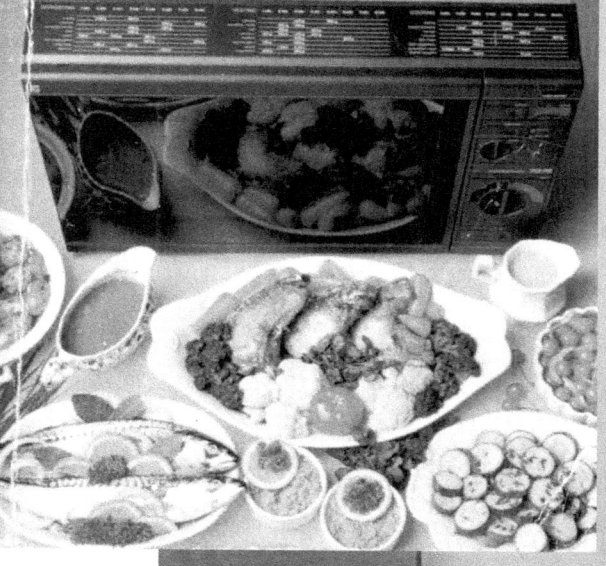

Look for the most bor-
ing book.

It makes complete
sense to hide your most
valuable or beautiful
things amongst the most
mundane or unattrac-
tive. I recall something
I heard as a child: when
breaking into a mansion
one should look behind
the ugliest painting to
find the household safe.
The flaw of that rule is
of course that the taste
of a burglar and a duke
may differ when it comes
to art.
When I was first invit-
ed to do this project
I began skimming my
book shelf. I found
various things used as
bookmarks, a ten dollar
bill, a twenty pound
note, and €320 hidden
so well that even I almost
could not find it. The
money was hidden inside
*Miller's Pocket Antiques
Fact File*. If you apply
my old burglar rule to
books, that's not a bad

choice. The
back would
small, oblo
er-bound, l
bit like a wa

I found an
Abe Books,
marketplac
ask their se
they've fou
They repor
similar to n
in by Miep
New Mexic
about a we
woman wh
left a large
tion behind
went to a lo
shop. Amo
was a micro
book which
out, contai
$1000 bills
"The book
chased by s
out of tow
idling away
waiting for
took the m
local bank
authenticit
was how w

choice. The only draw-
back would be that it's
small, oblong and leath-
er-bound, looking a little
bit like a wallet.

I found an article where
Abe Books, an online
marketplace for books,
ask their sellers what
they've found in books.
They report on a story
similar to mine. It is sent
in by Miep in Carlsbad,
New Mexico and it tells
about a wealthy, elderly
woman who died and
left a large book collec-
tion behind. Most books
went to a local thrift
shop. Among them
was a microwave cook-
book which, as it turned
out, contained forty
$1000 bills.
"The book was pur-
chased by someone from
out of town who was
idling away the time
waiting for her ride. She
took the money to a
local bank to verify its
authenticity and that
was how we heard about

it. She didn't give a cent back to the thrift shop, either. A deeply frustrating experience for many, I can assure you." Considering $1000 bills were last printed in 1934, they are very collectible and worth far more than their face value, so the buyer of the used cookbook actually got over $40,000.

A microwave cookbook. That must be one of the safest titles for hiding something in these days. Even too good for the passed-away owner of the forty $1000 bills. If you're hiding something extra precious you can even speculate as to which recipes are safer than others. What's the chance you will navigate to "Chocolate Sauerkraut Cake" or "Ham and Bananas Hollandaise" when you want a treat?

As printed books become less popular in favour of more hi-tech ways of reading such as e-readers, "spritzing," etc., they will become even safer hiding places, but what interests me is what might be the microwave cookbook of the future? Could it be *Minecraft: The Ultimate Guide, Windows 8.1 For Dummies or iPhone: The Missing Manual?* Or perhaps a contemporary food fad like a Paleo cookbook or a book of recipes for the NutriBullet "The Worlds Most Powerful Nutrition Extractor"? Time will tell. I'm sure people of the 70s thought microwave cooking was there to stay.

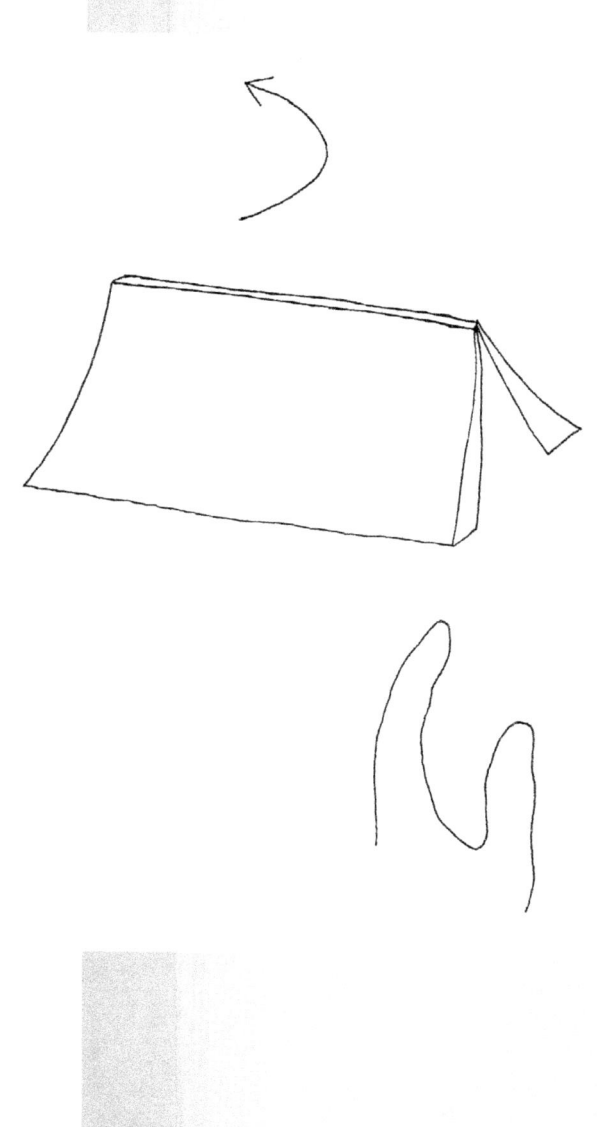

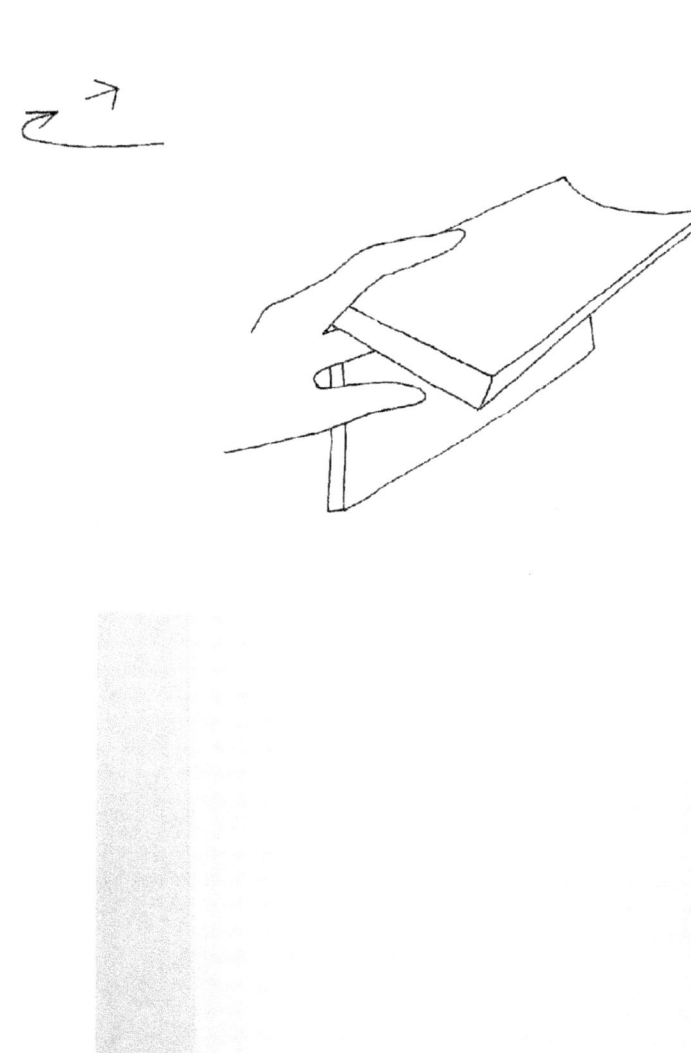

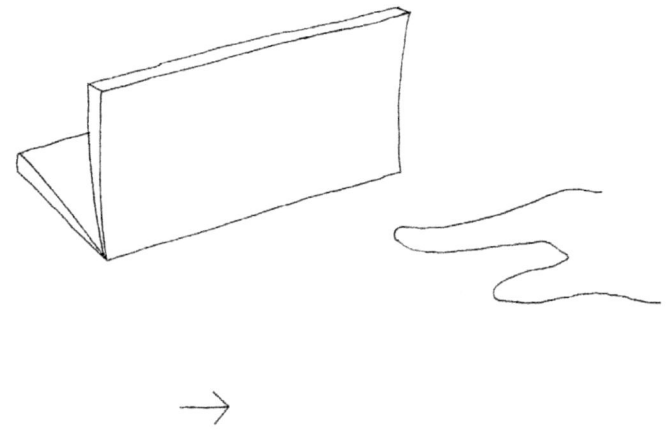

→

A set of keys in your hand and just when you're about to fall asleep your fingers relax and the keys drop to the floor. The noise wakes you up, the keys have fallen already. You have to get down and pick them up.

I walk around, fly around, drive around, I call around. Everywhere passing through and stopping by, and the blank book is with me. It grows and shrinks depending on where I am and how I need it.

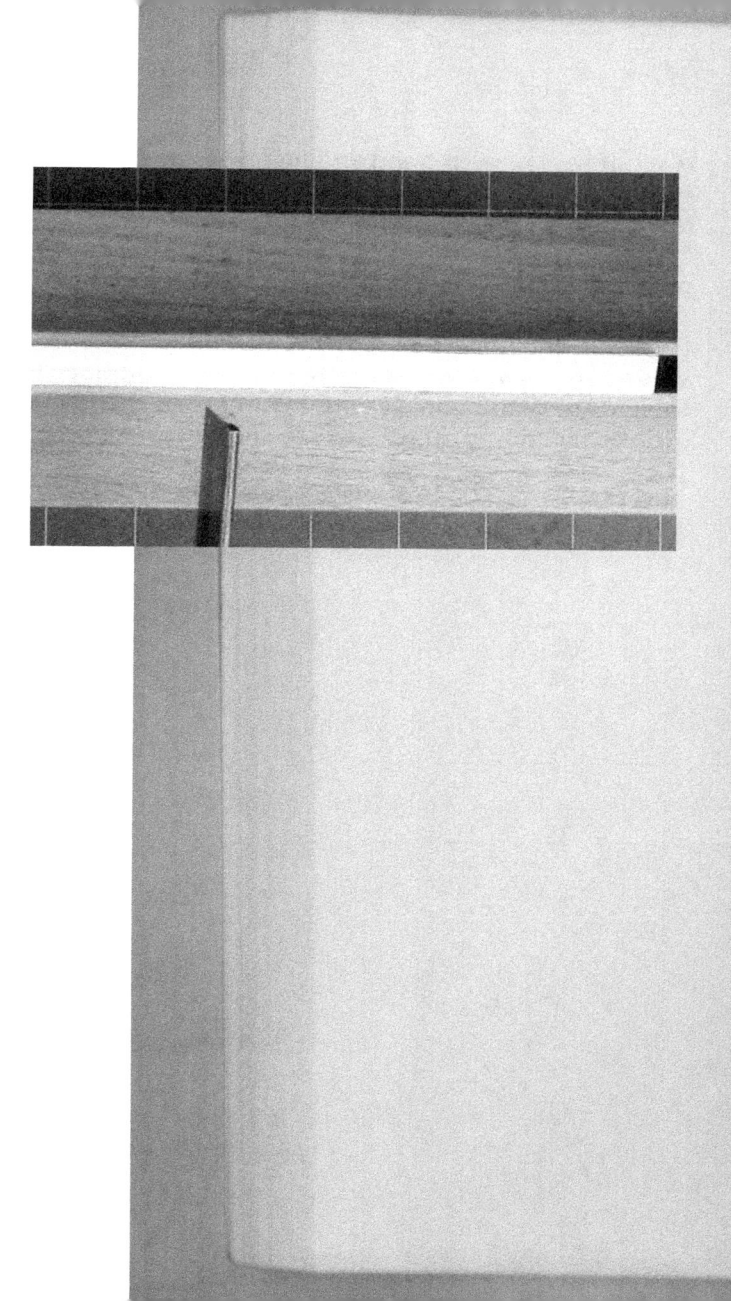

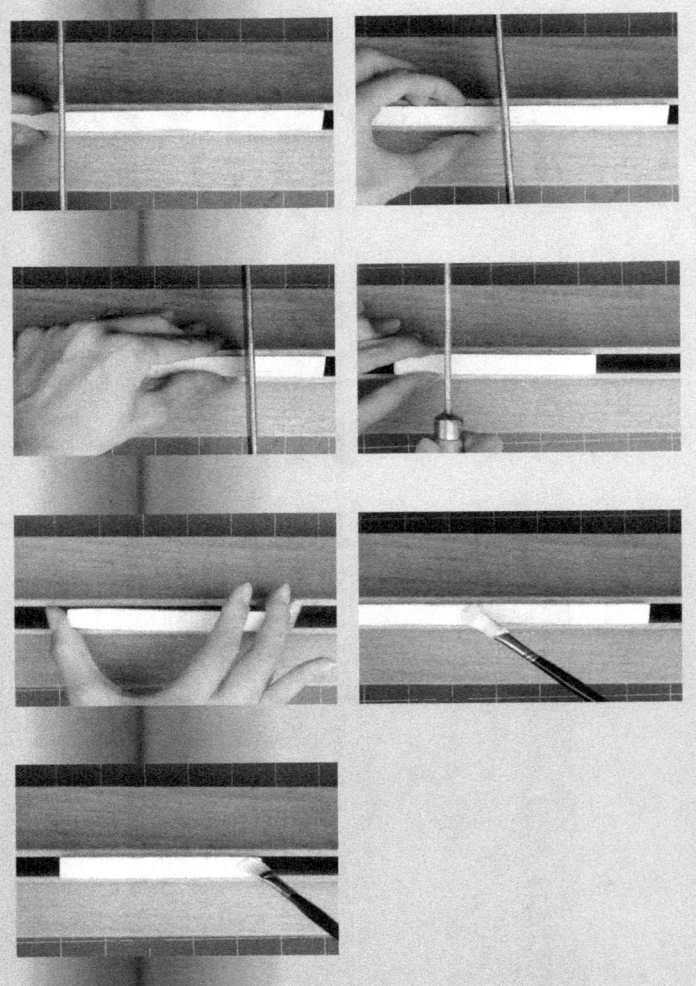

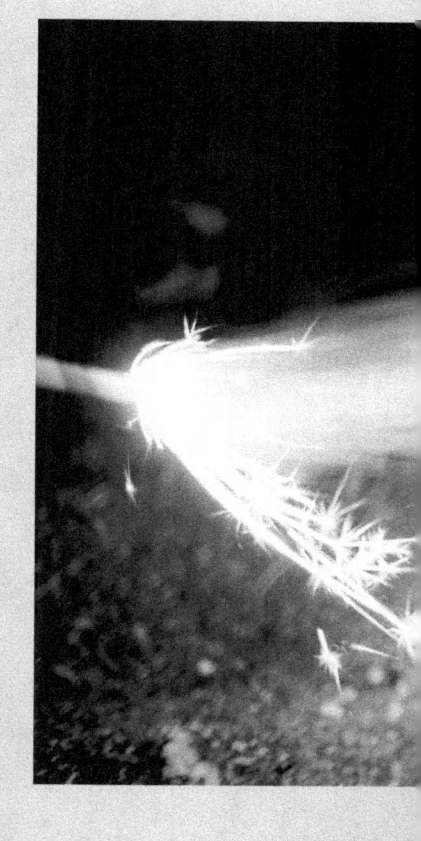

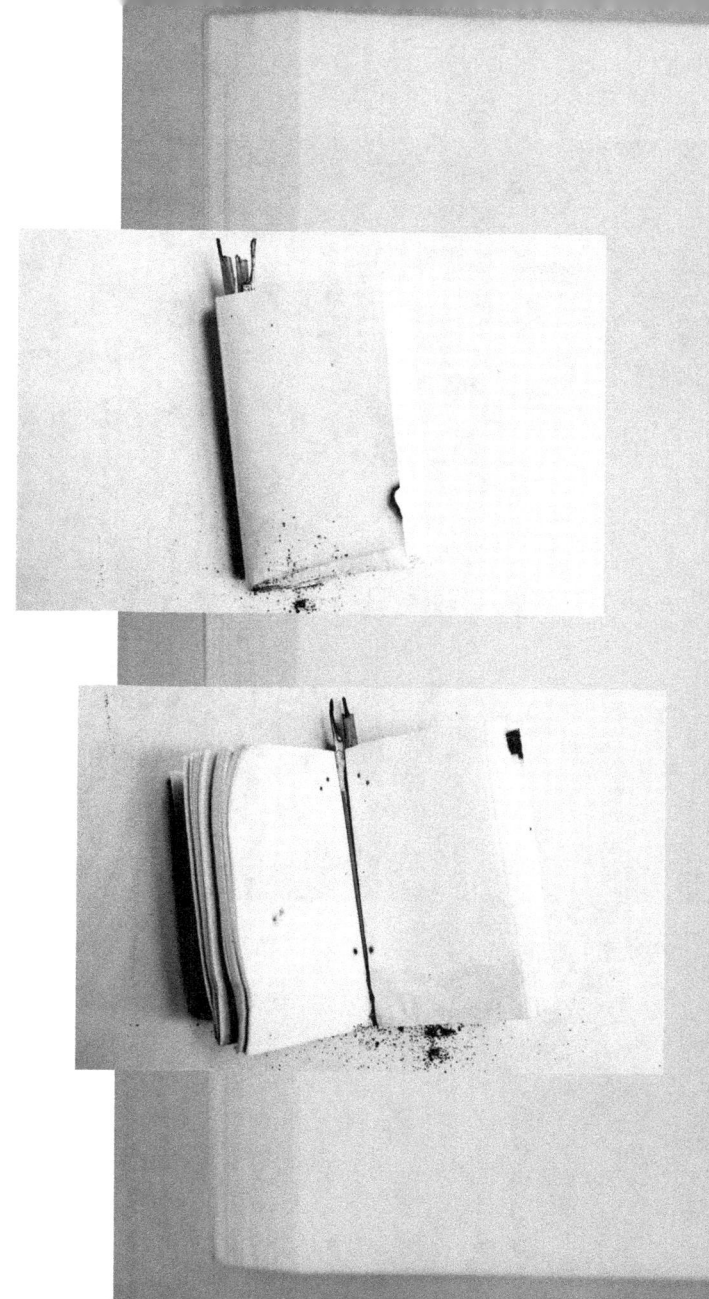

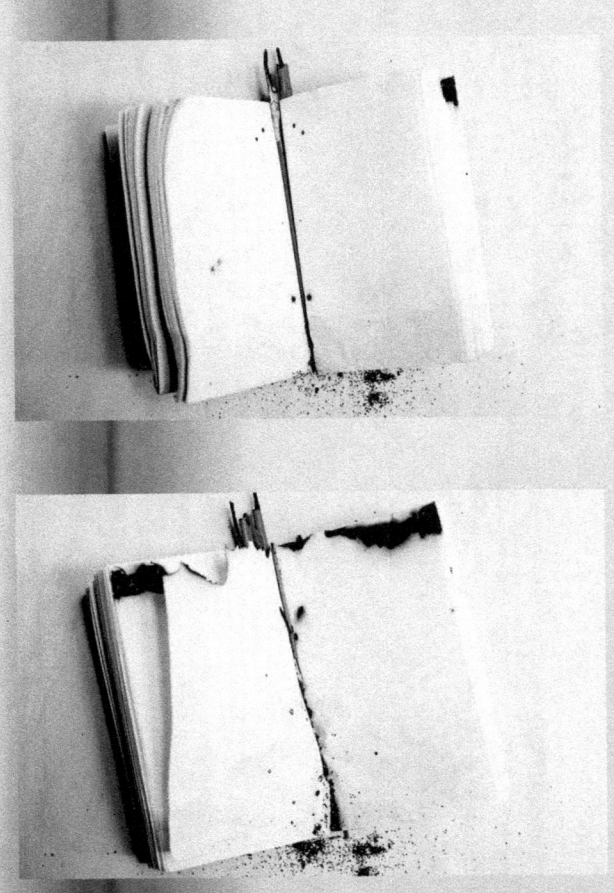

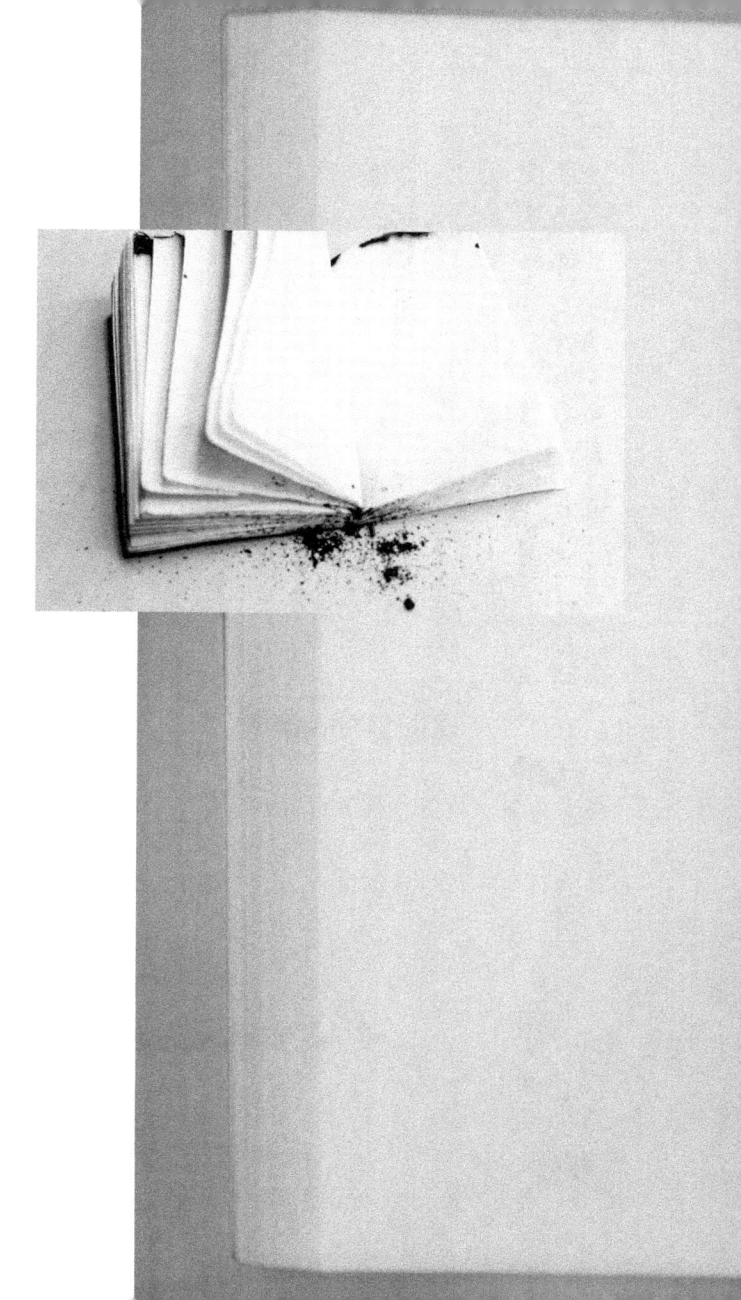

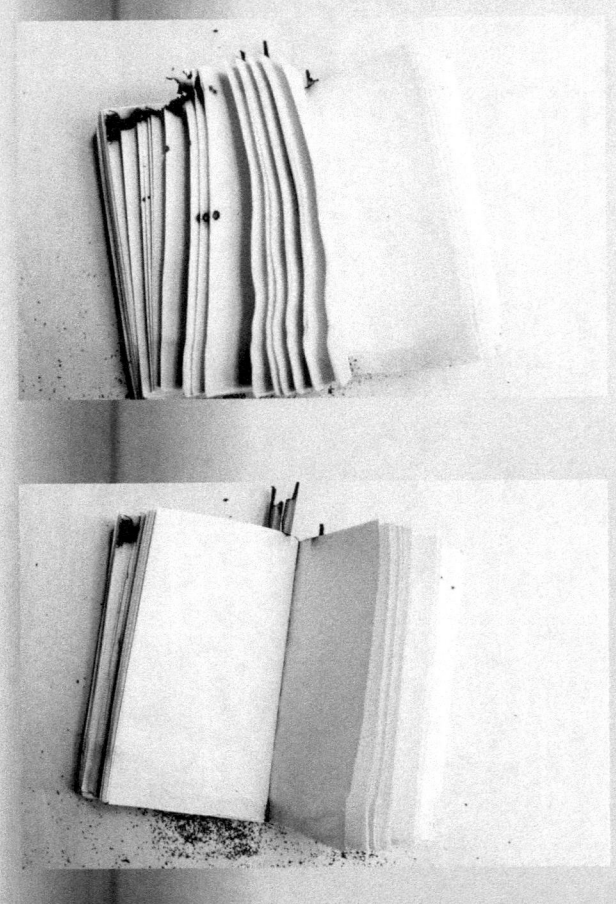

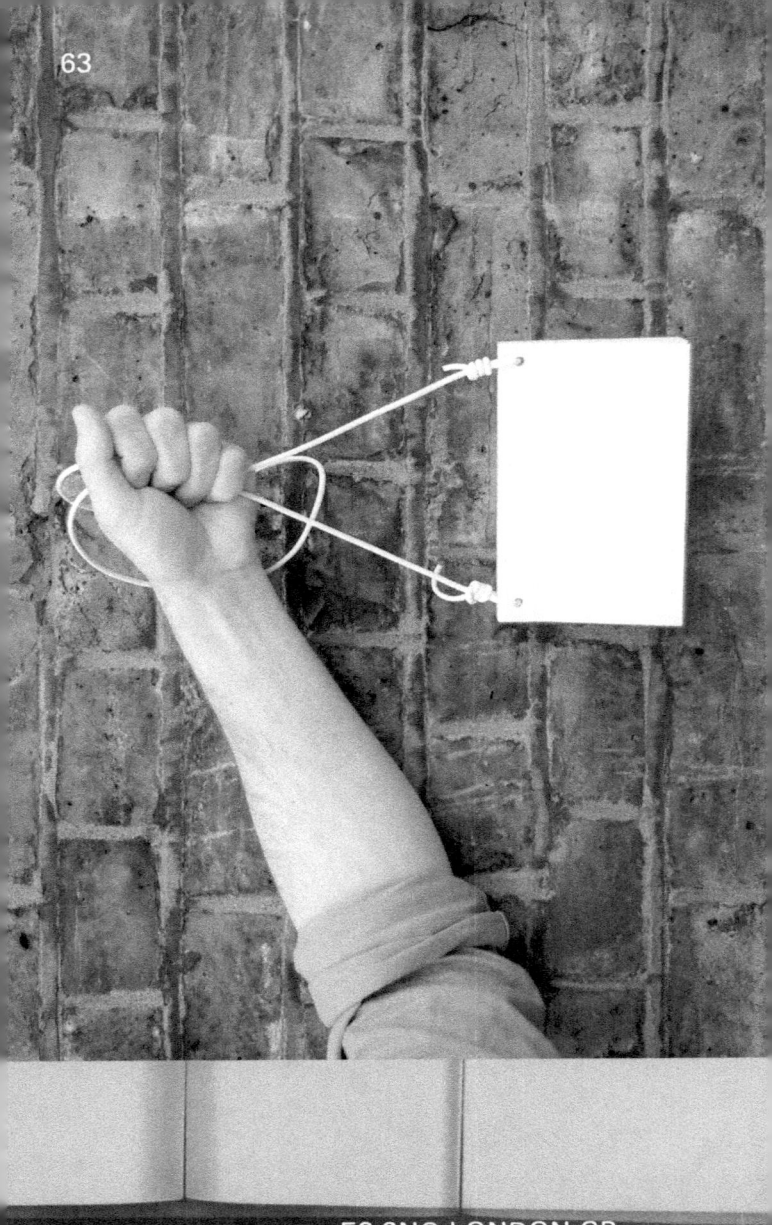

4.4625 m²

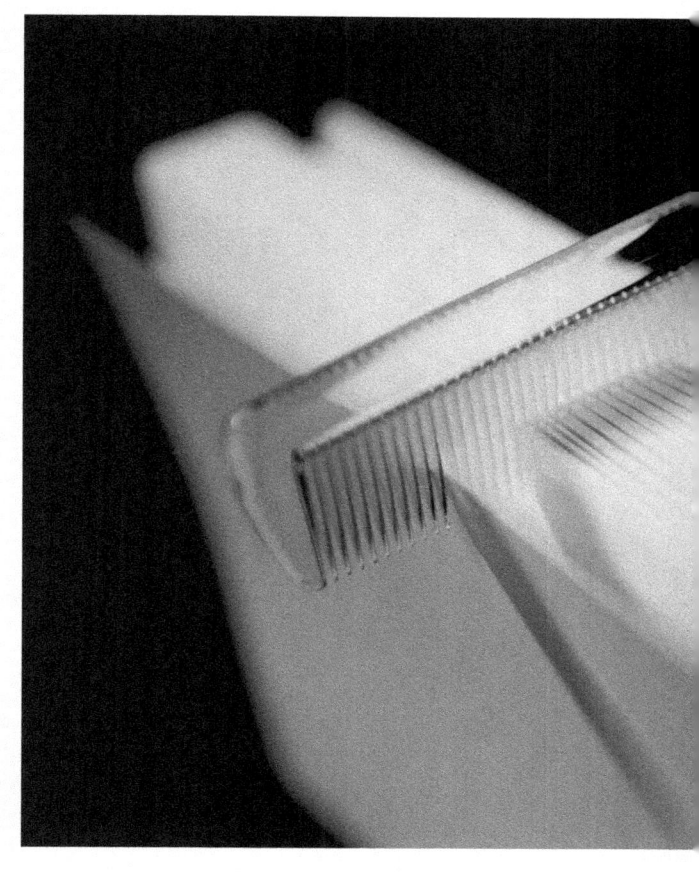

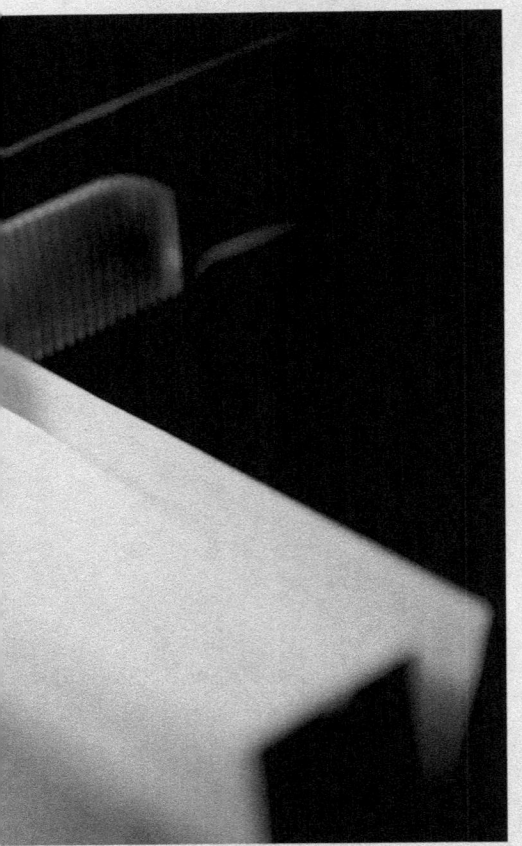

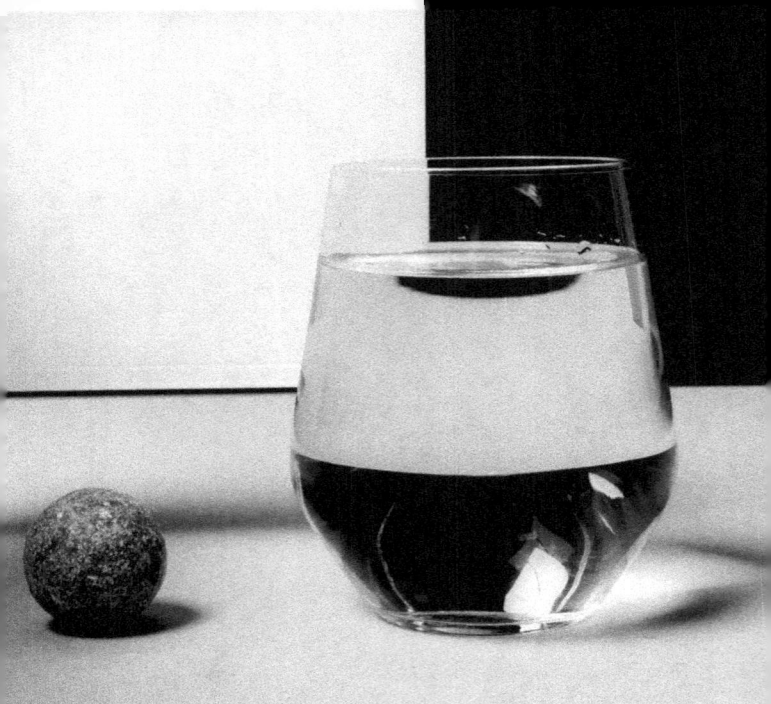

93170 BAGNOLET FR

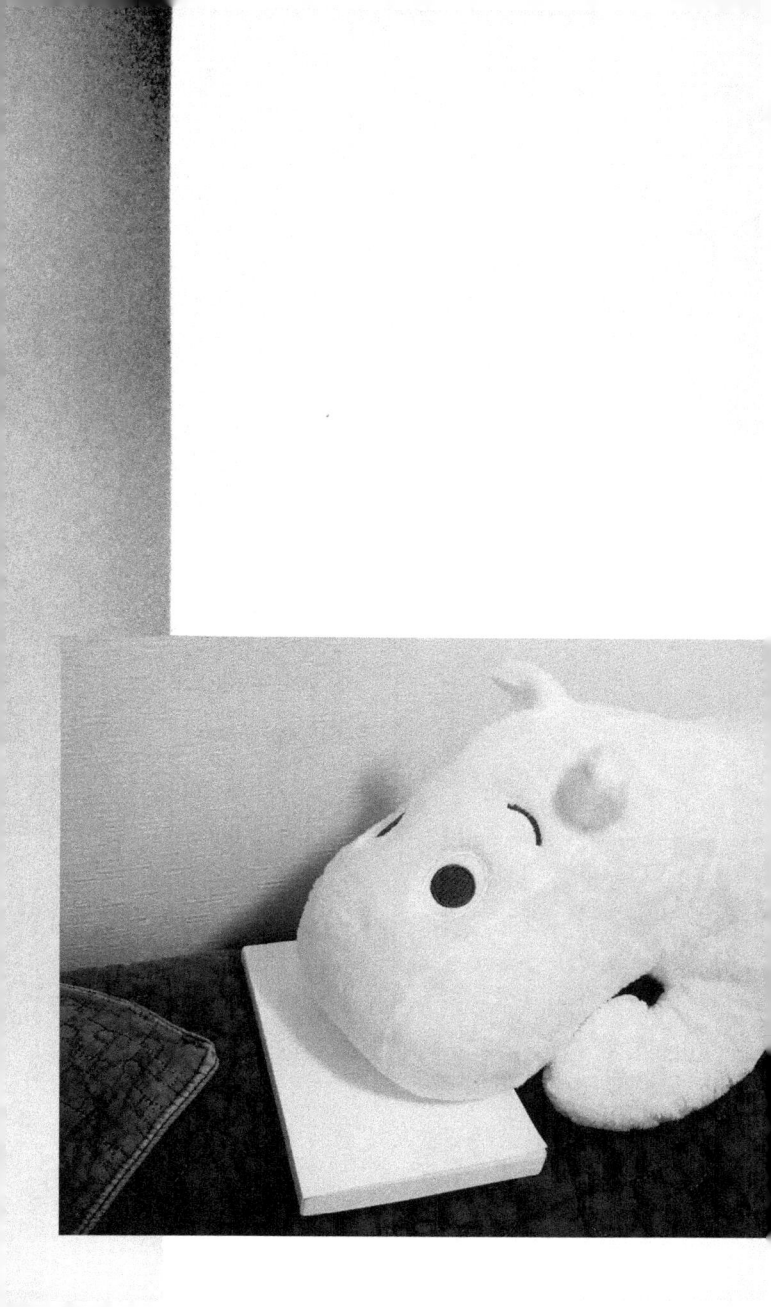

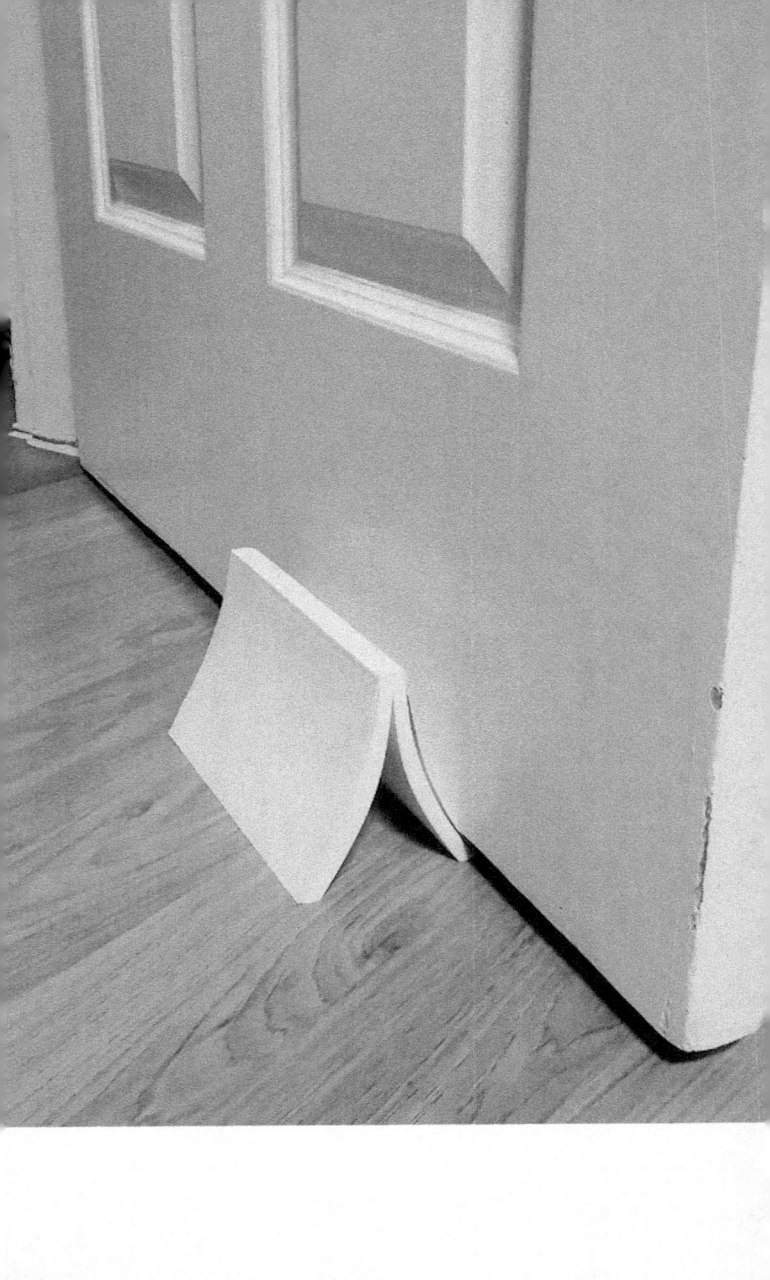

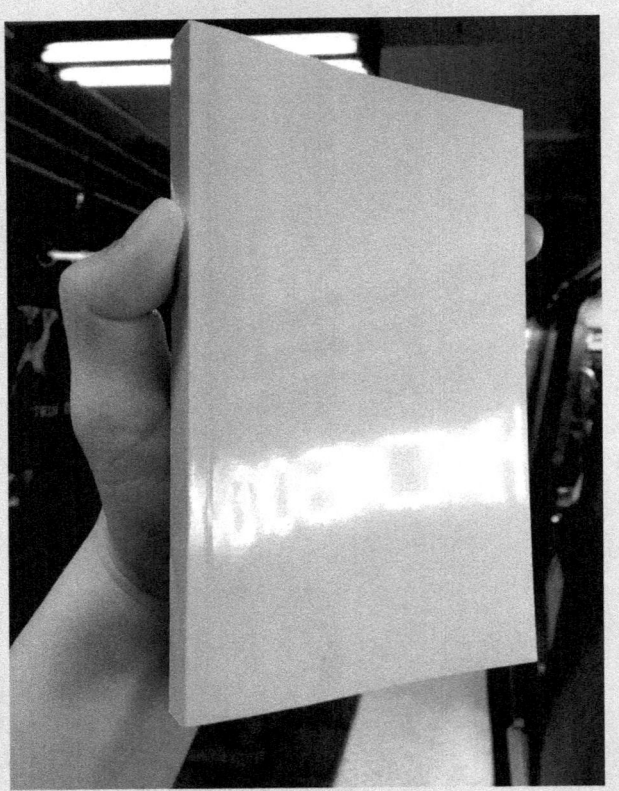

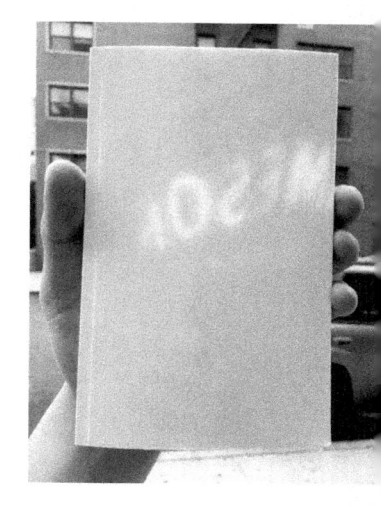

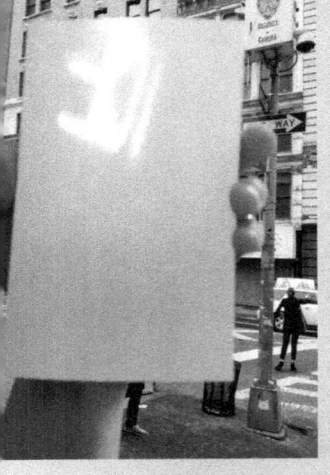

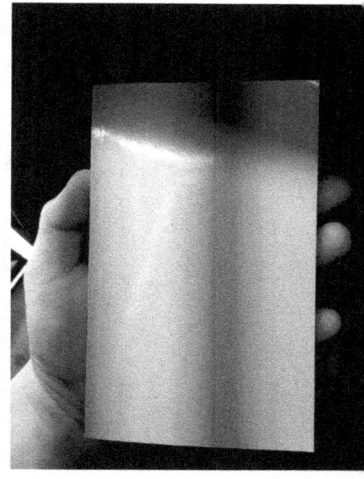

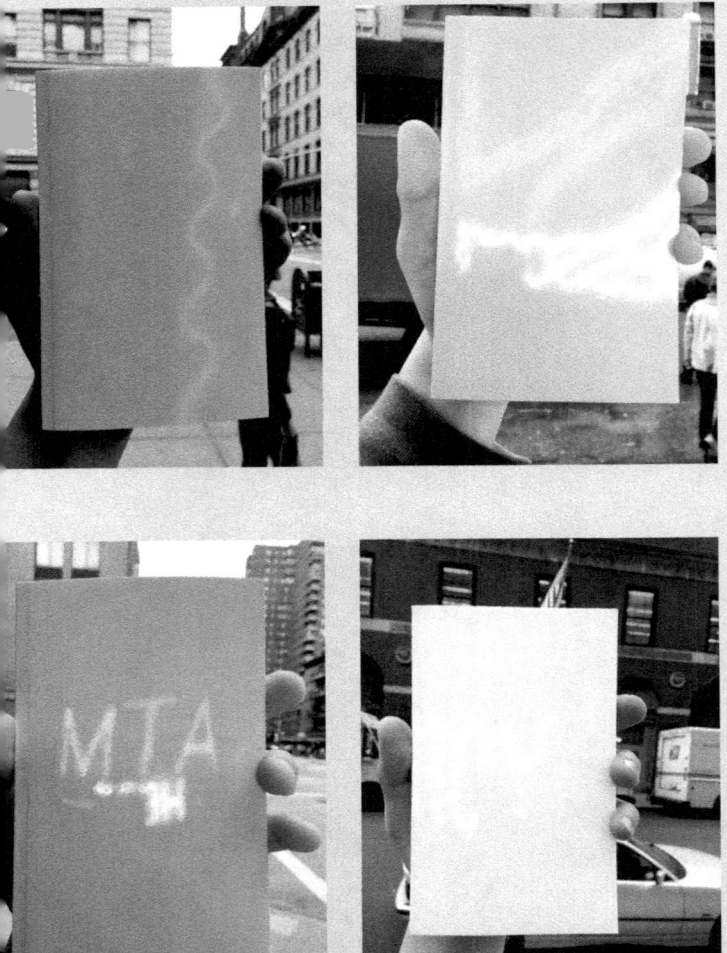

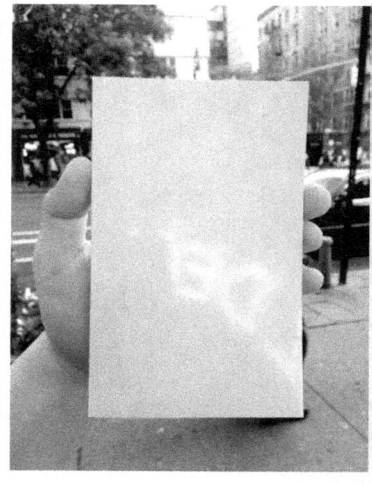

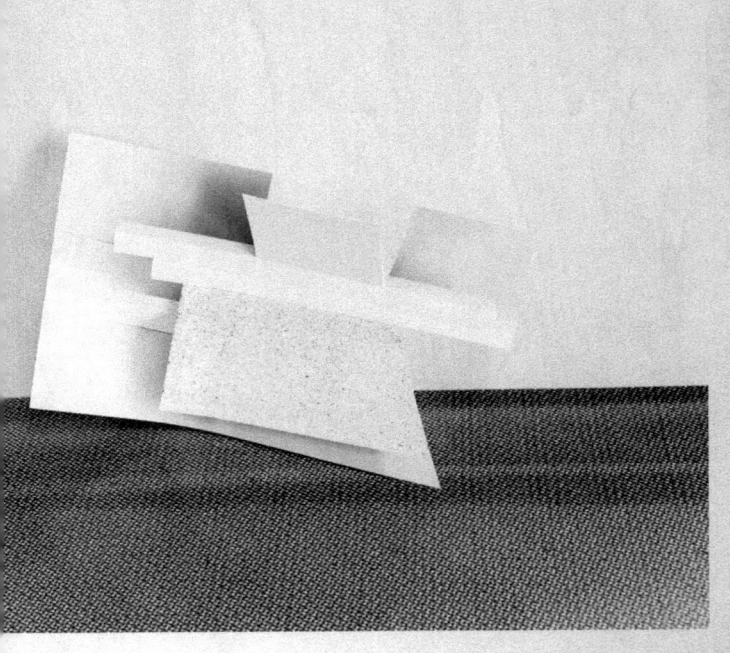

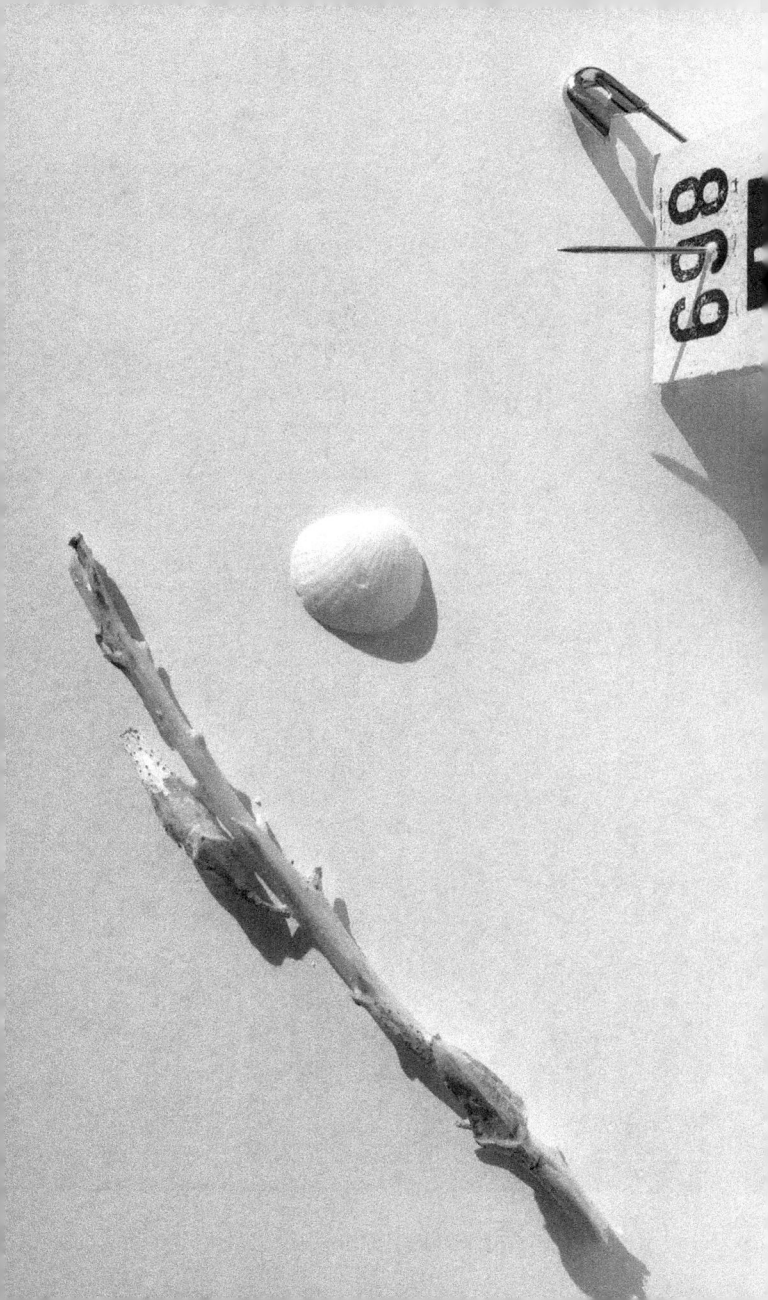

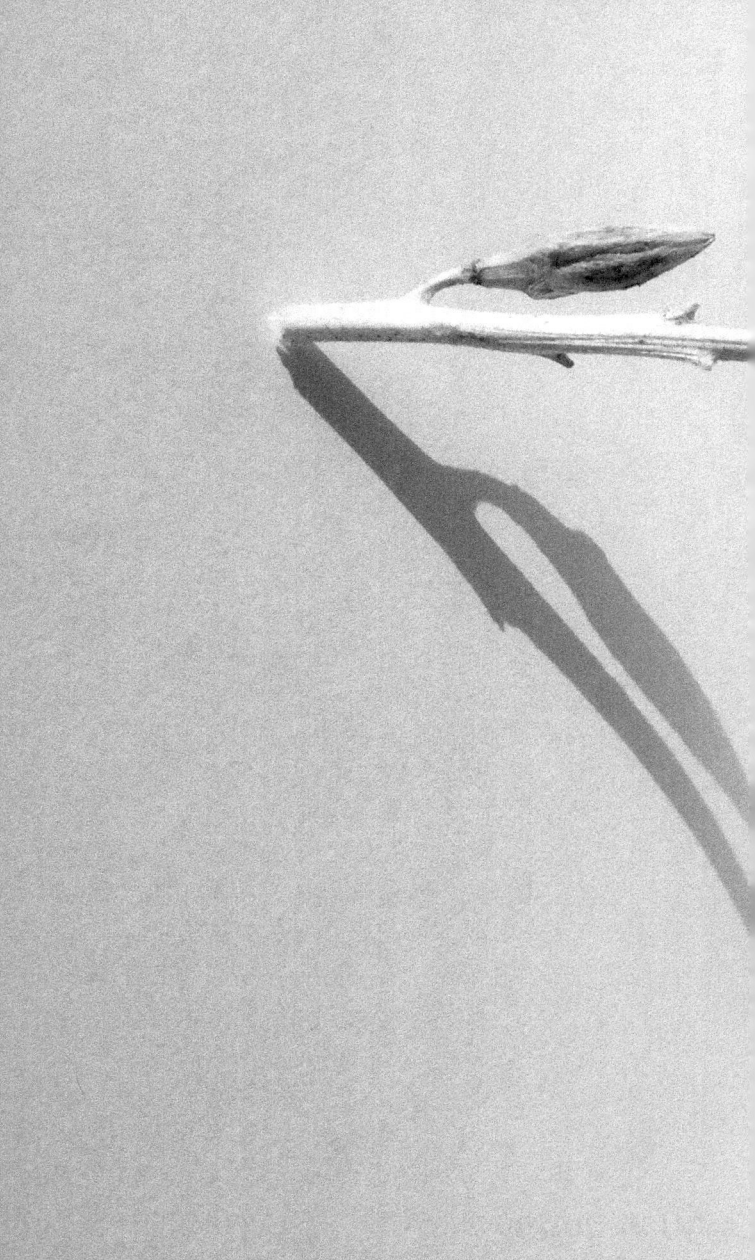

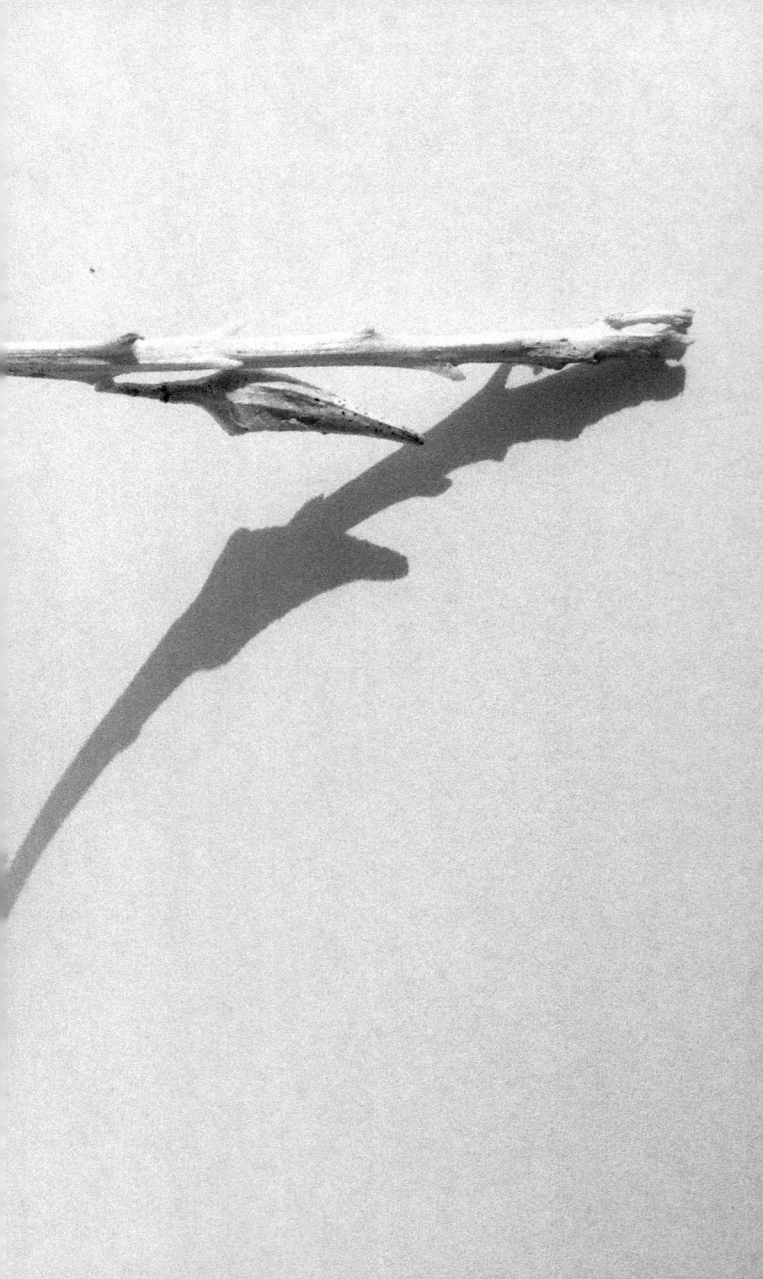

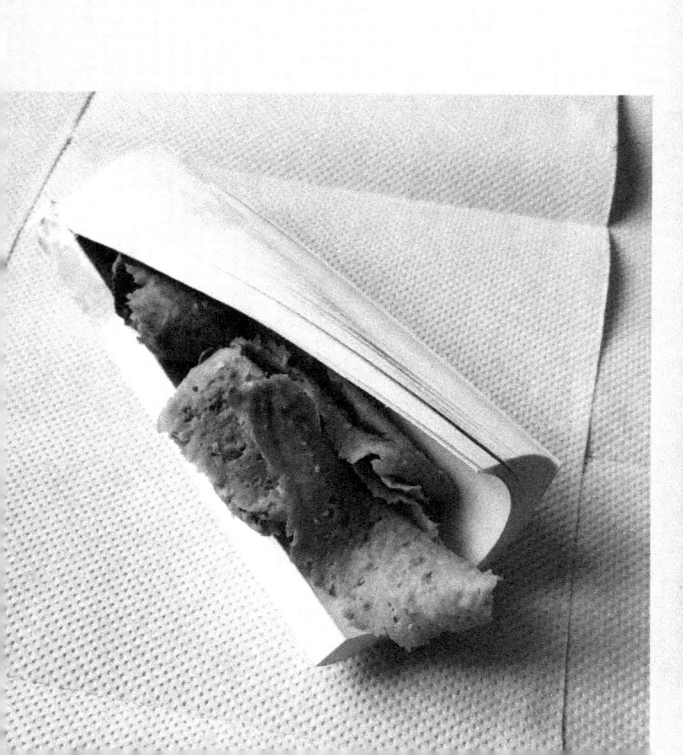

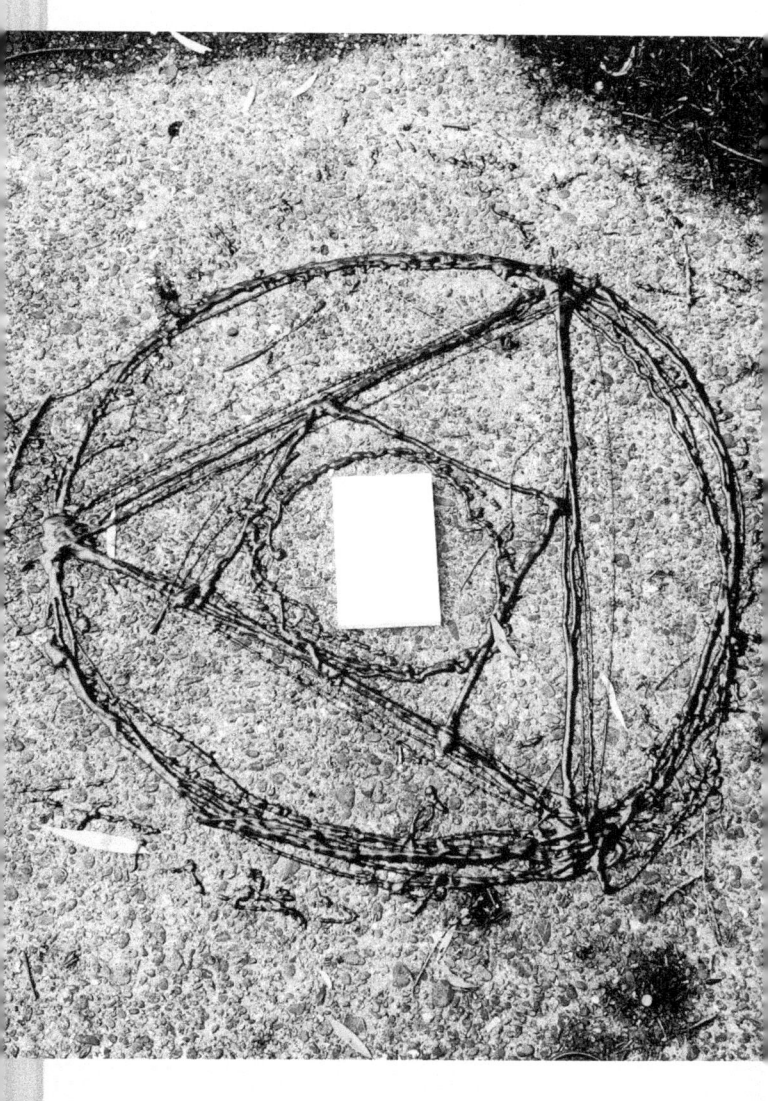

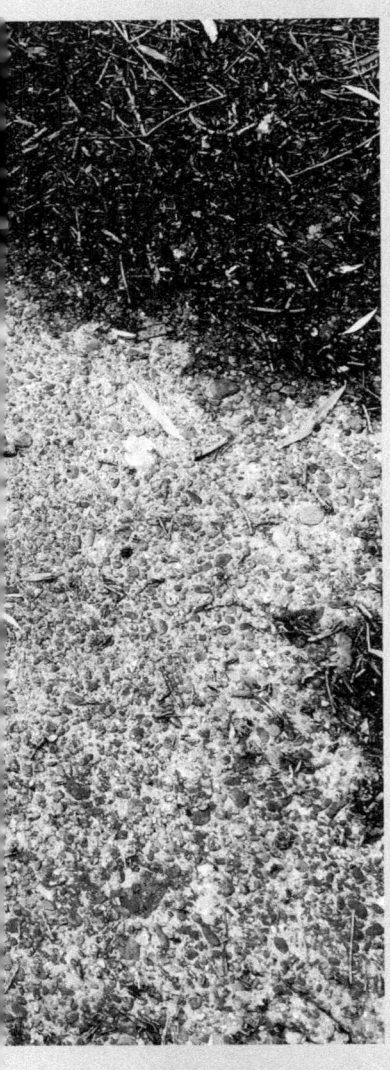

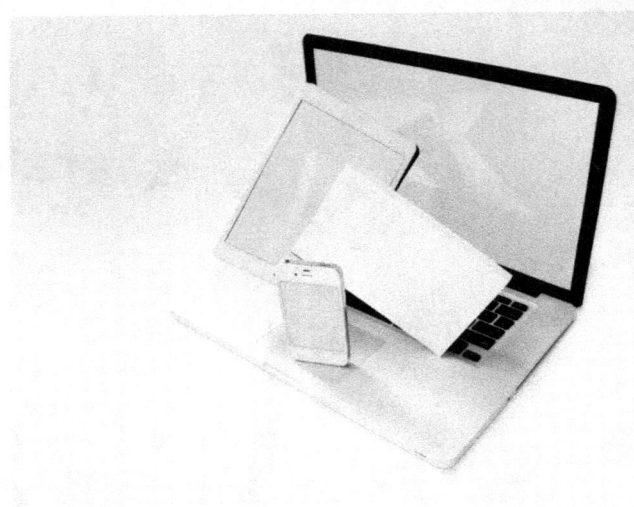

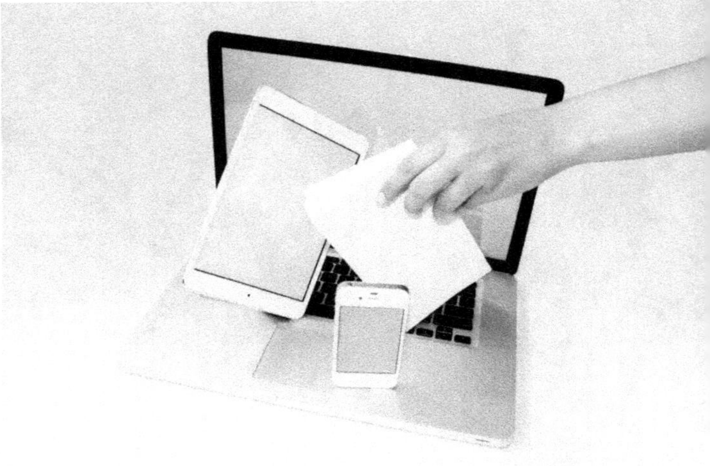

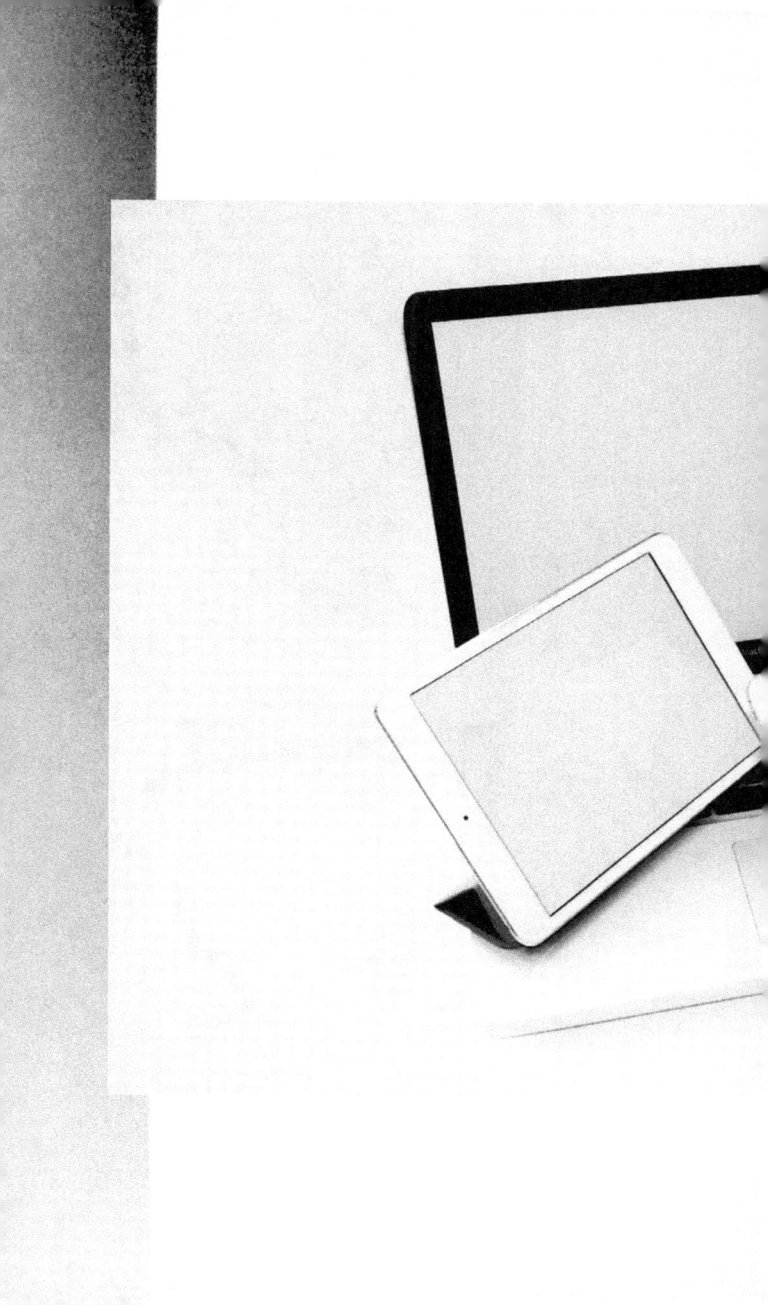

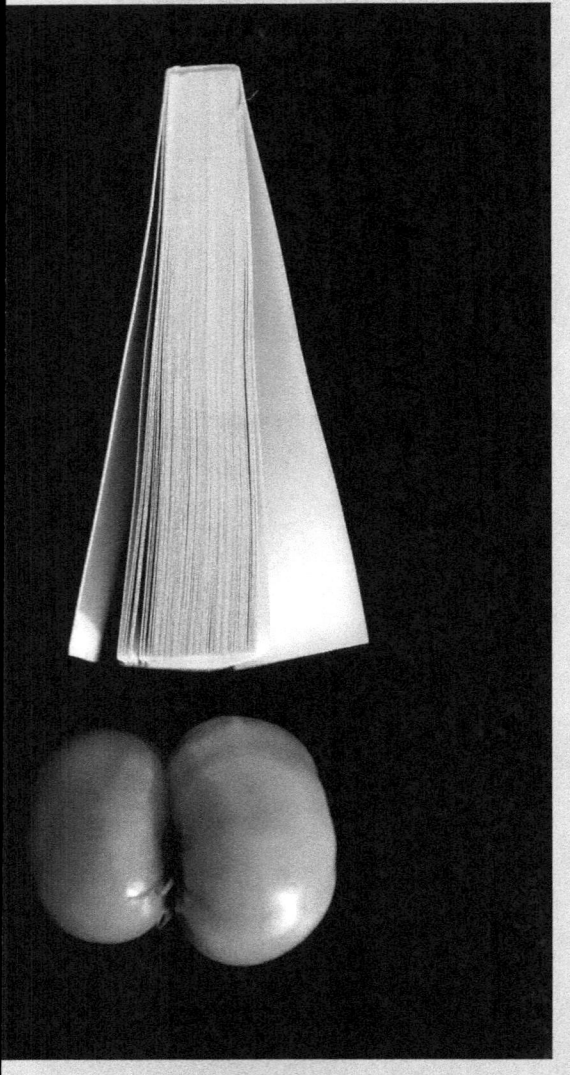

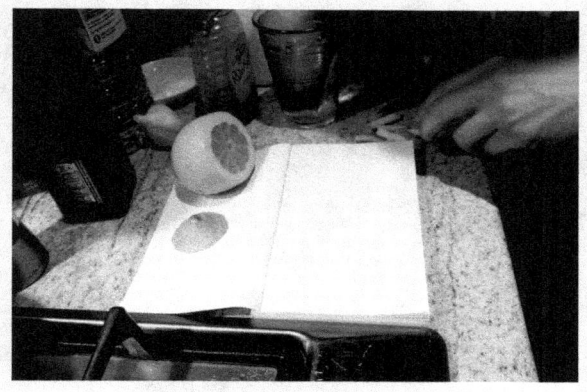

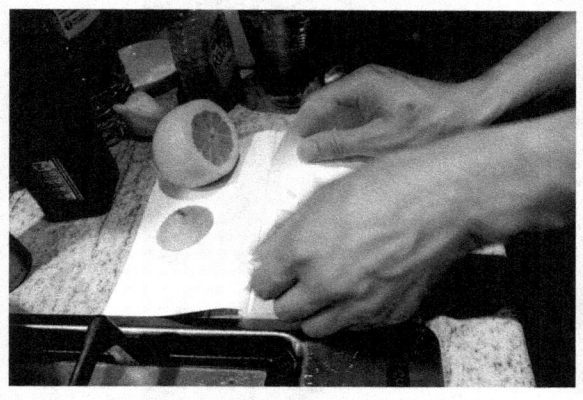

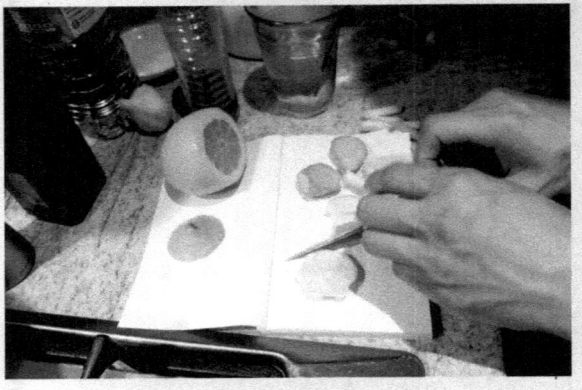

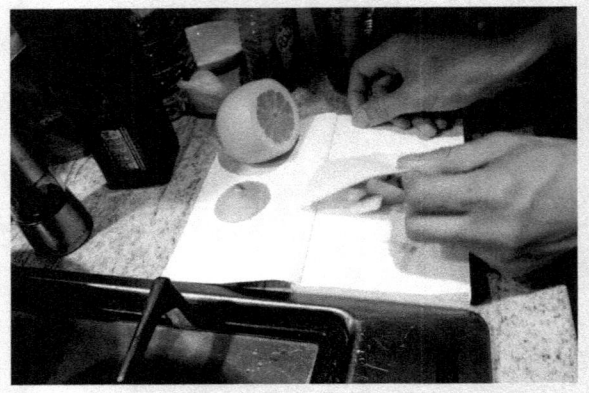

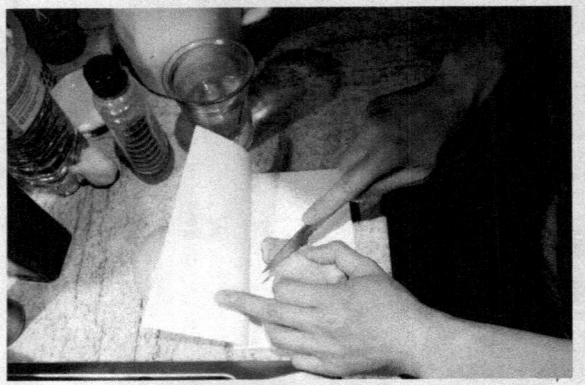

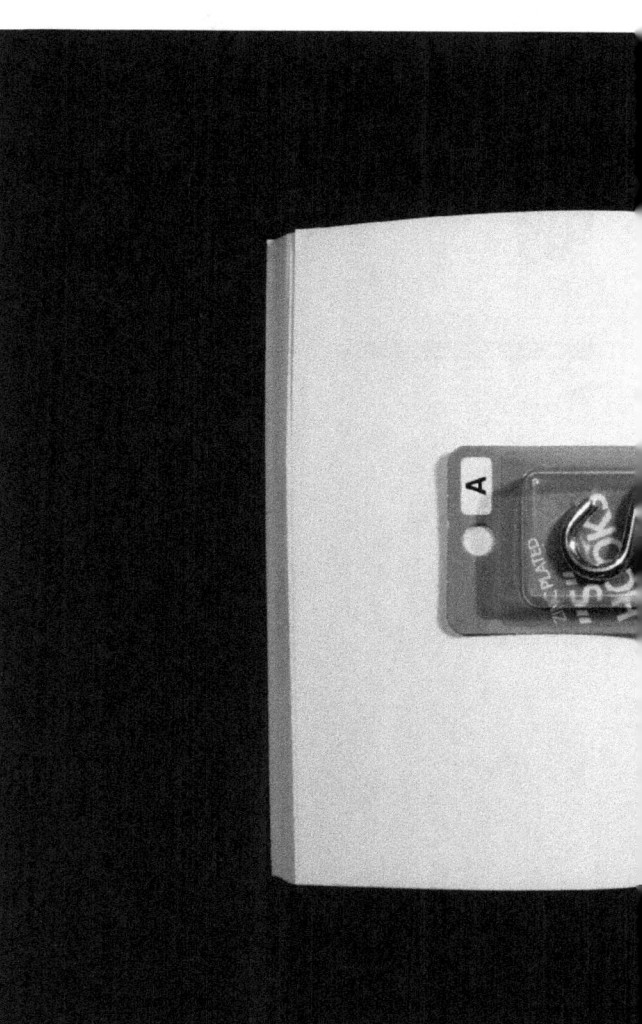

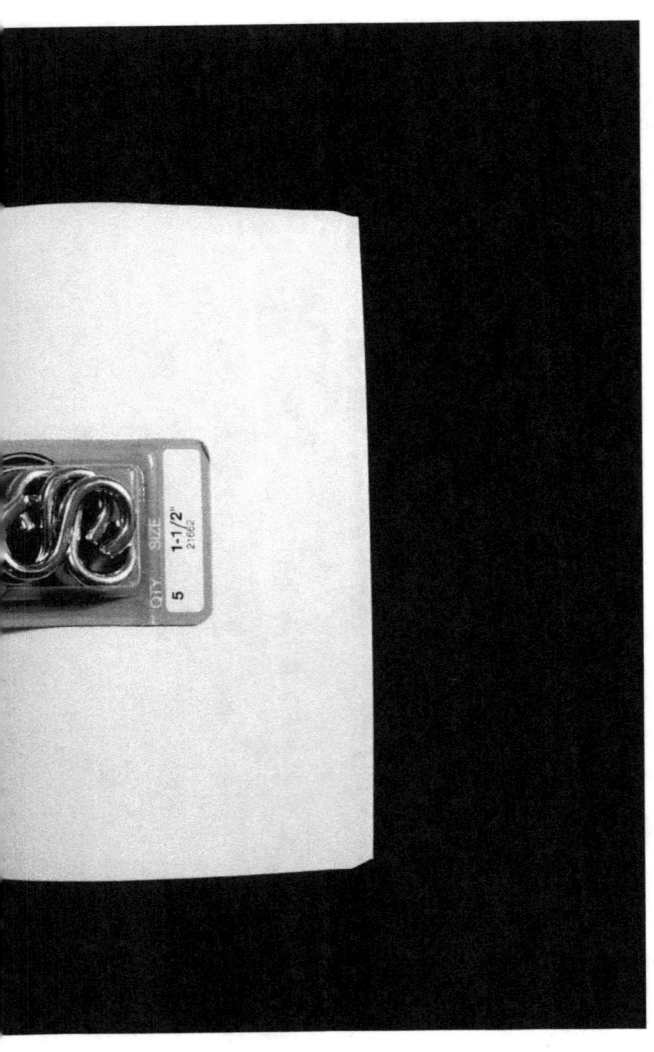

QTY. SIZE
5   1-1/2"
2162

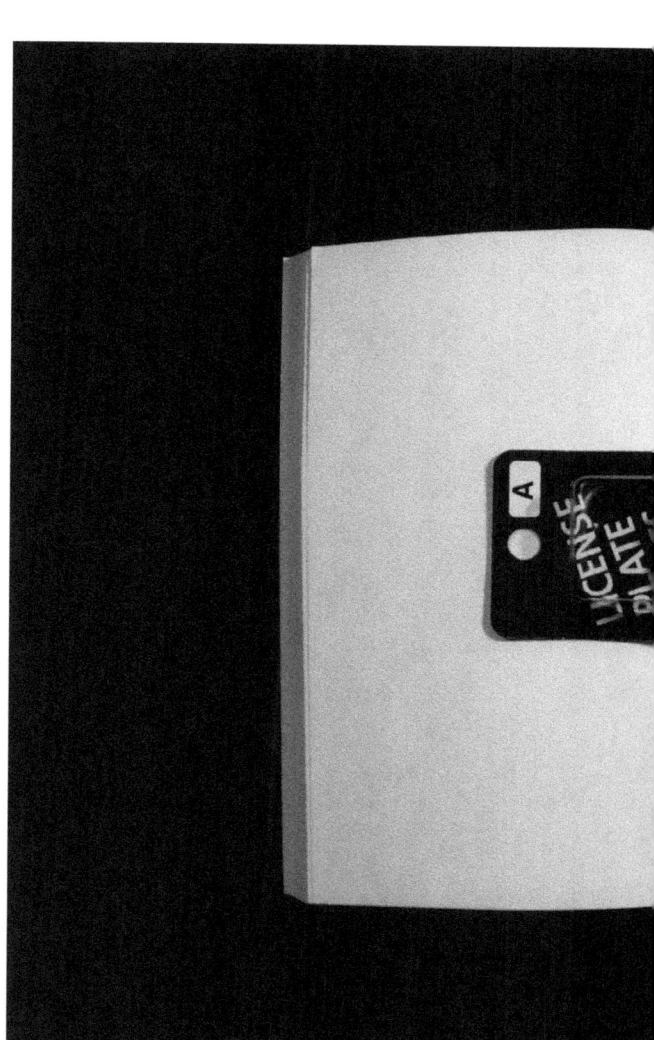

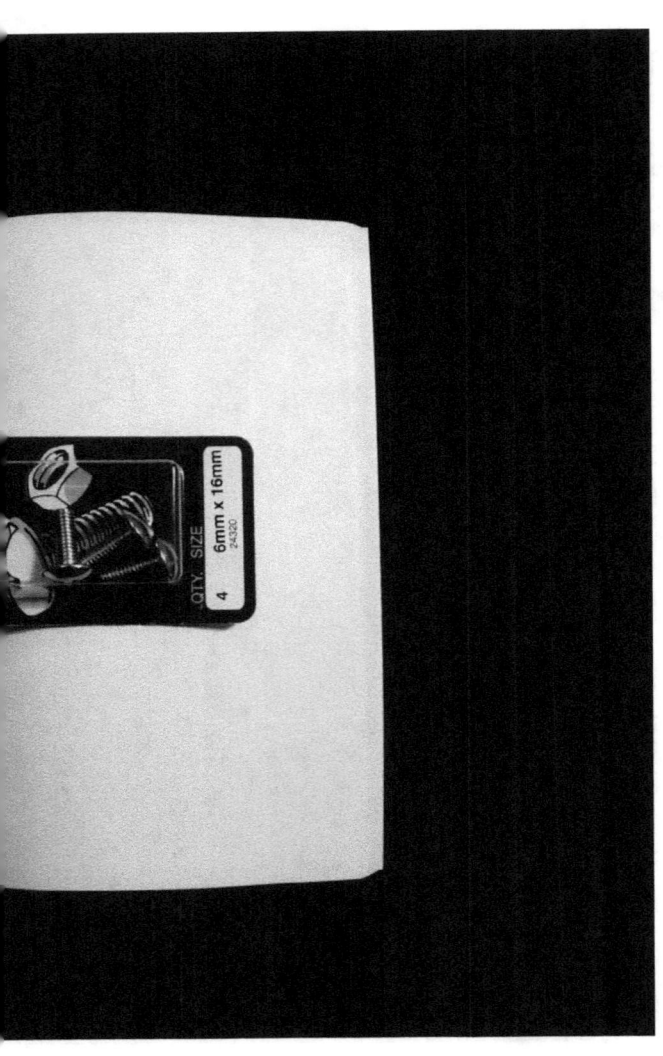

QTY. SIZE

4 **6mm x 16mm**

24320

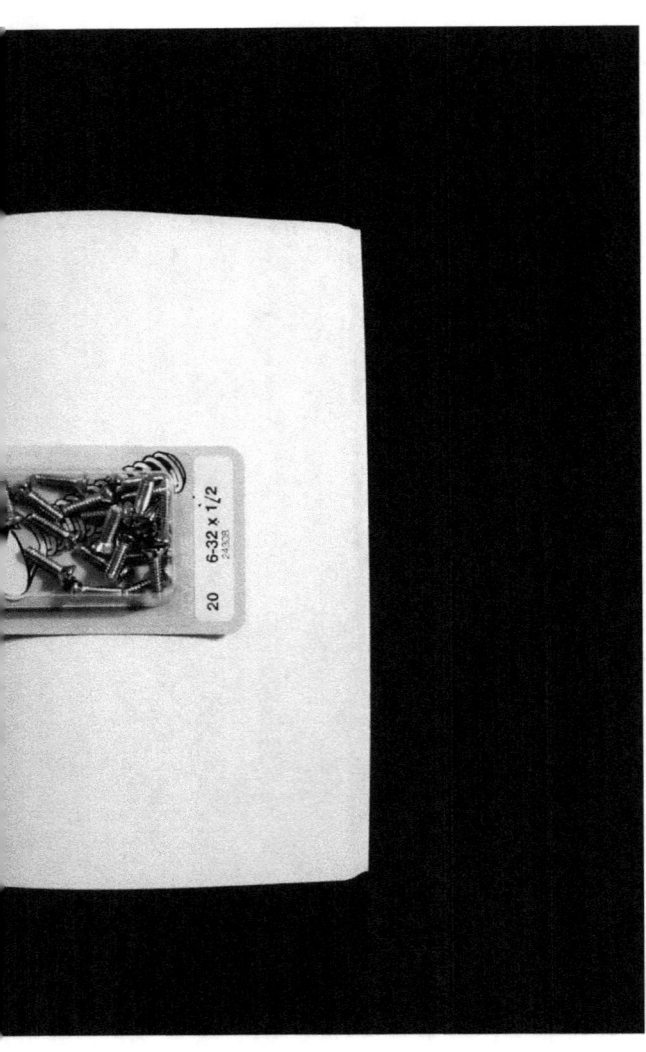

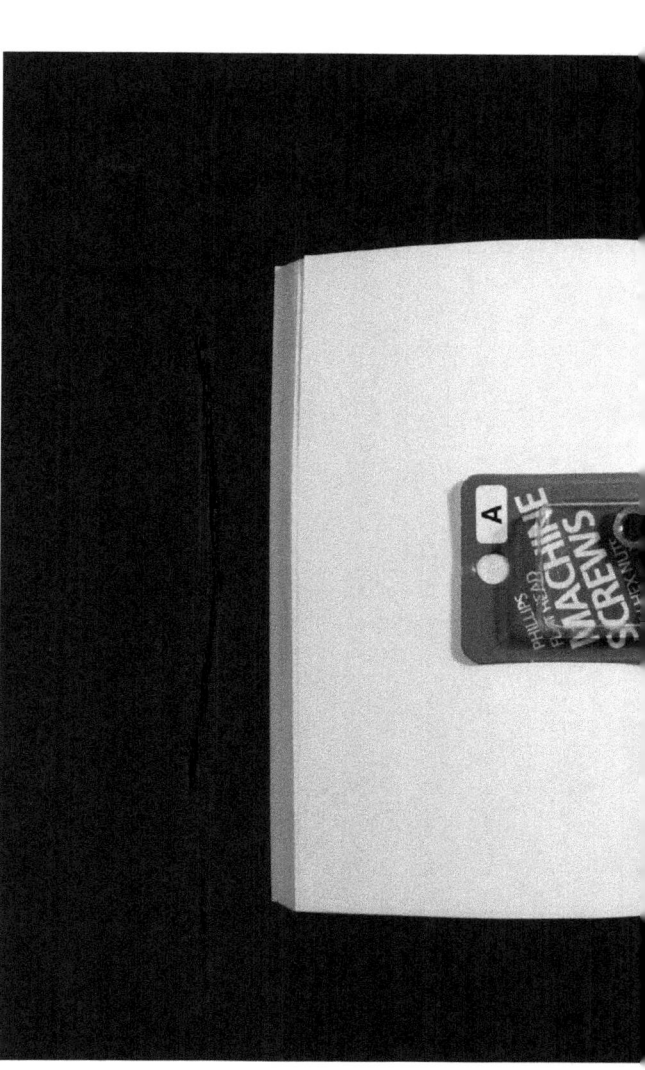

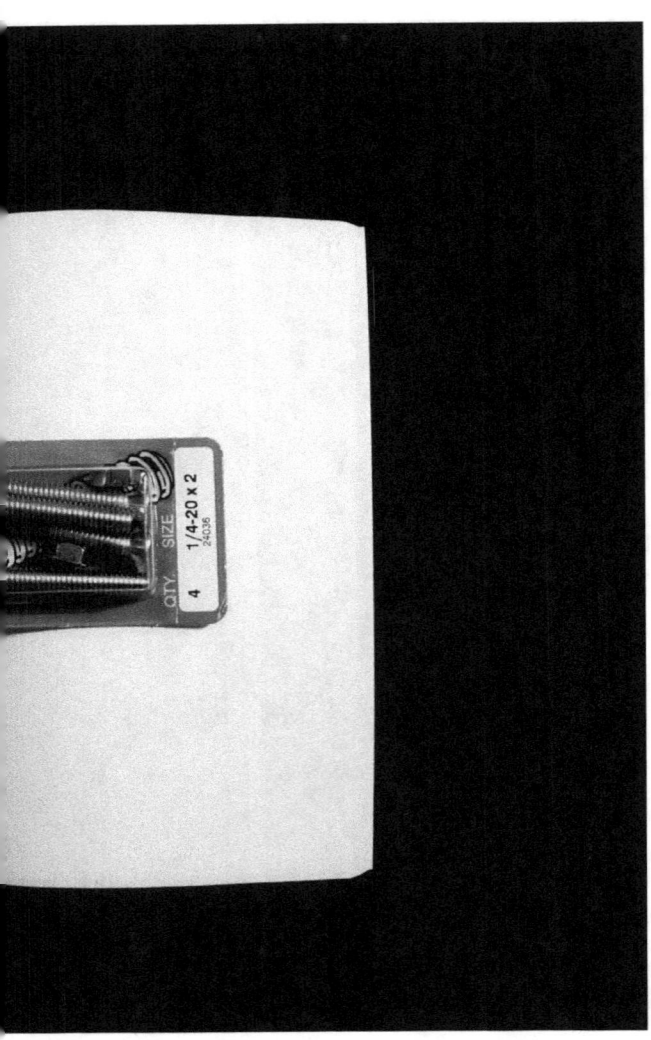

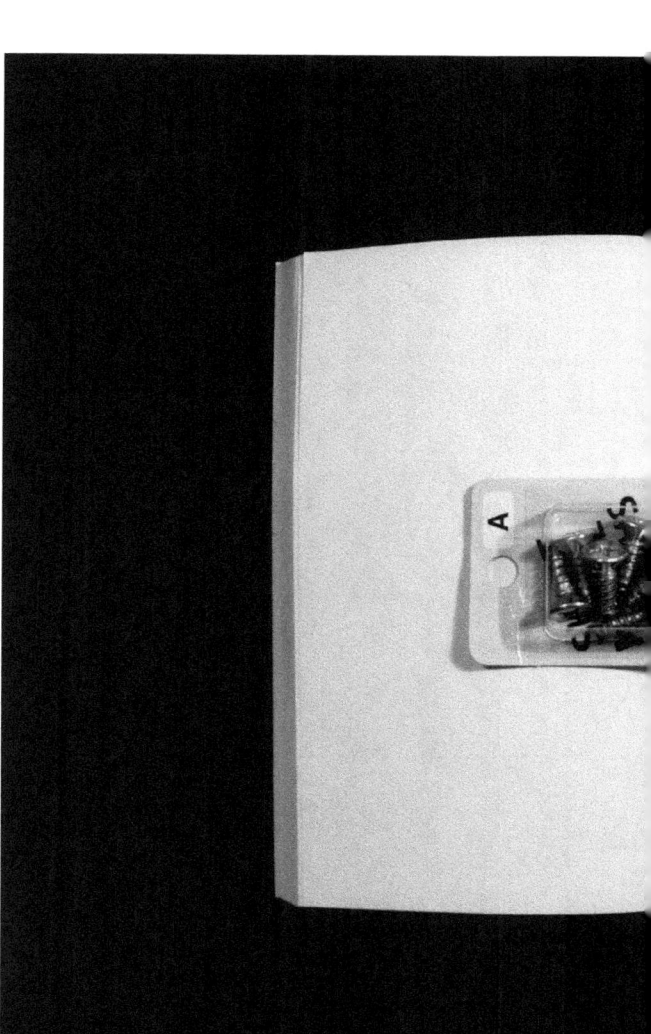

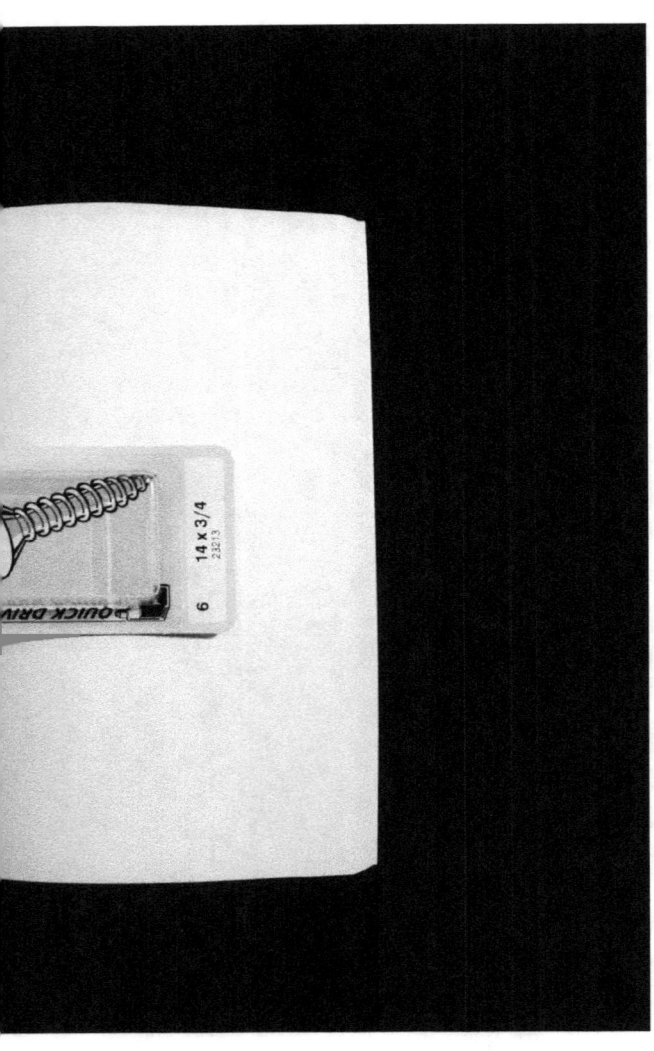

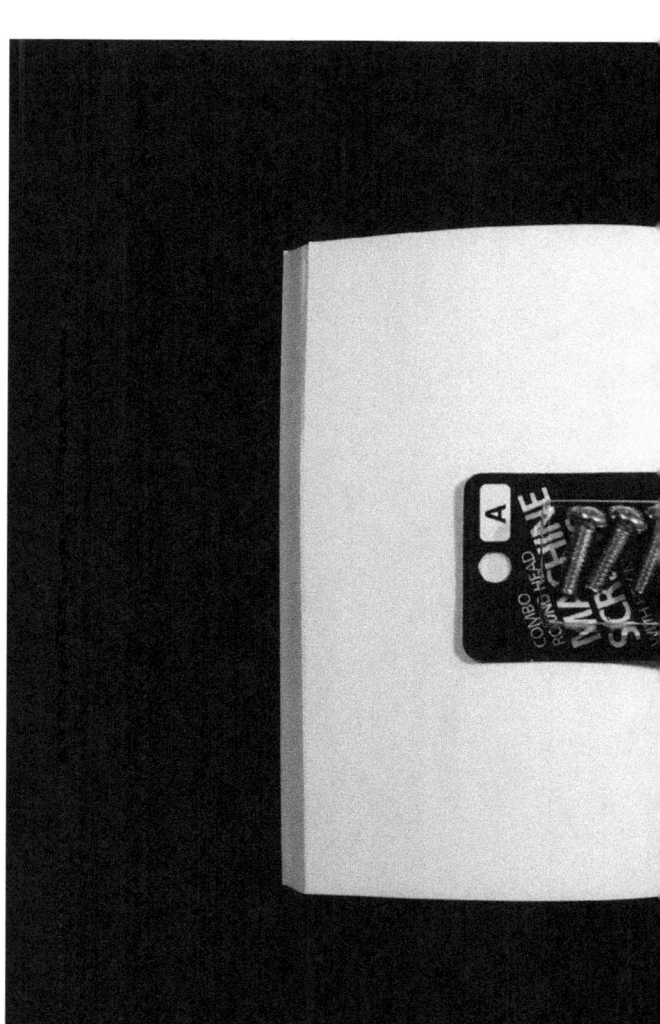

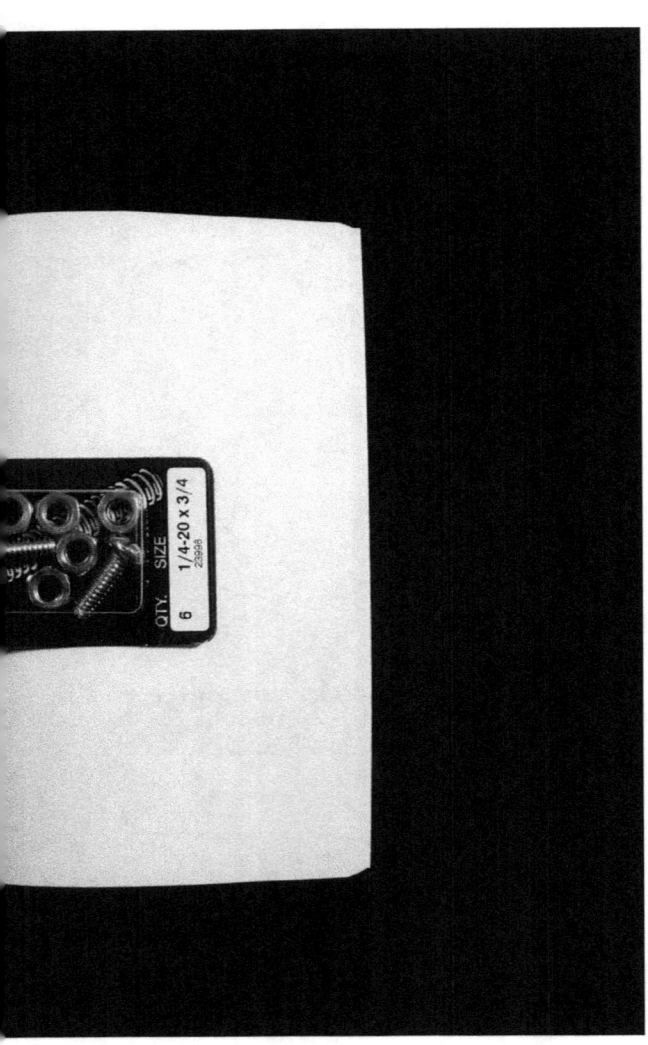

習後

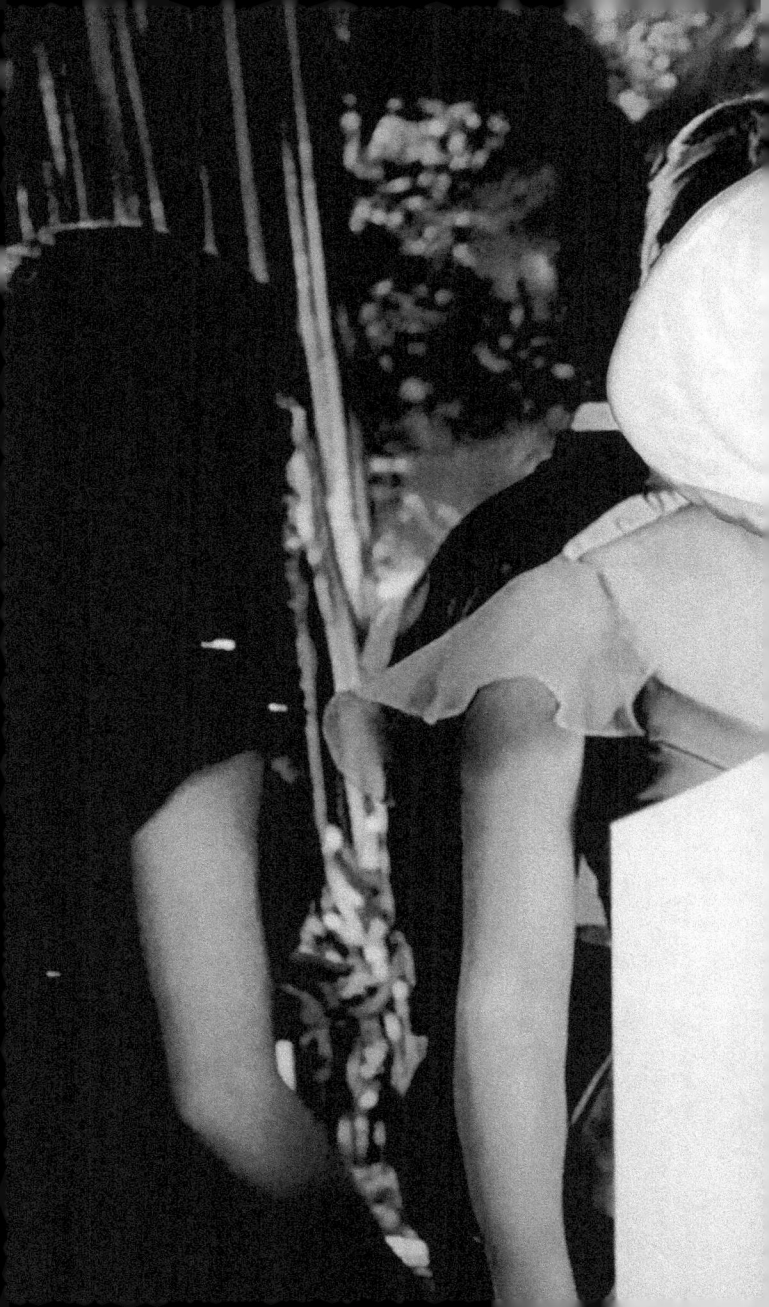

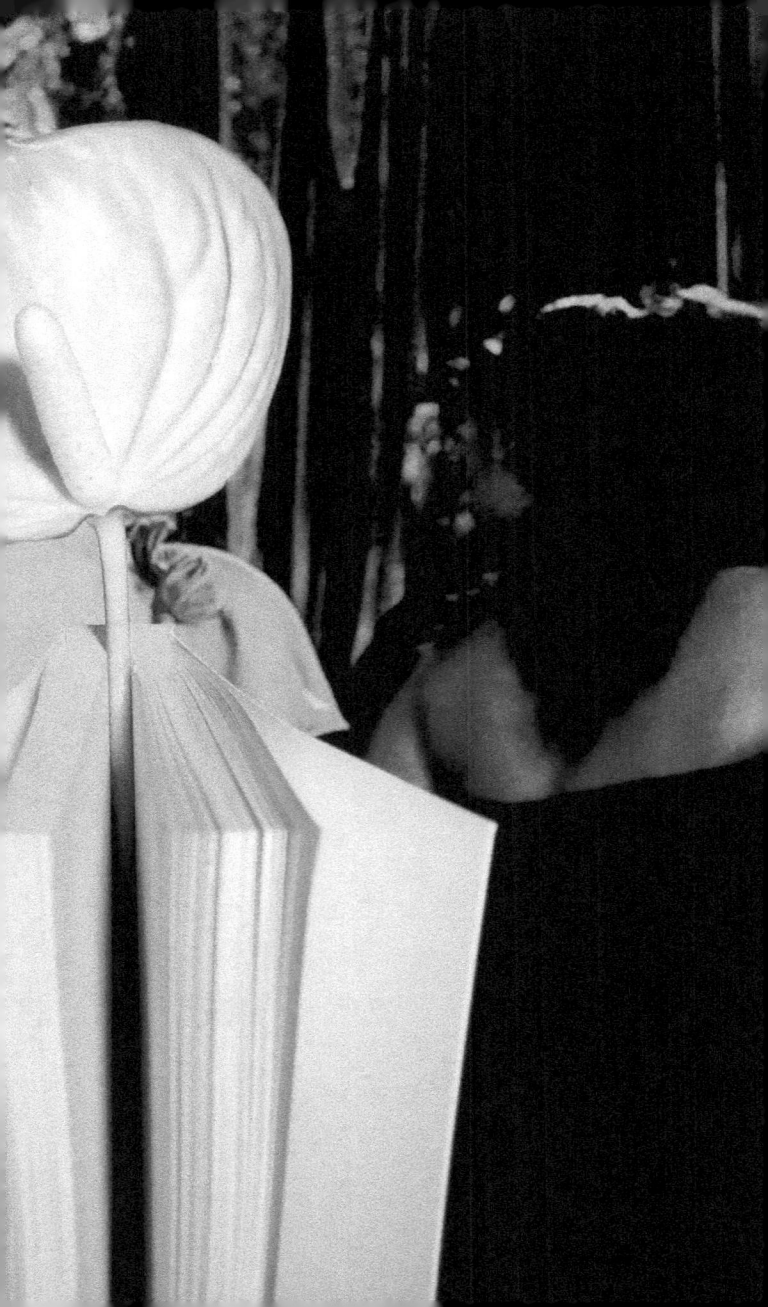

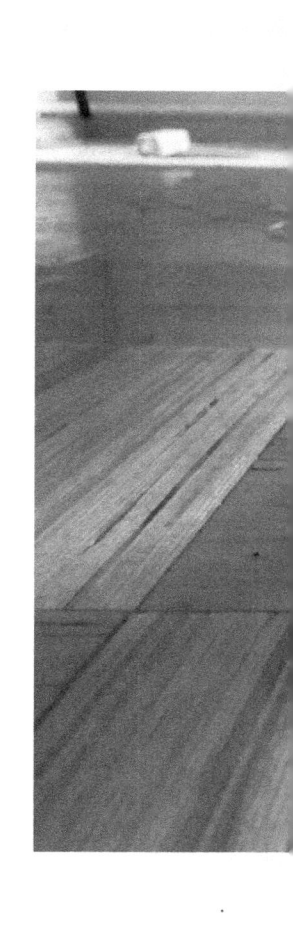

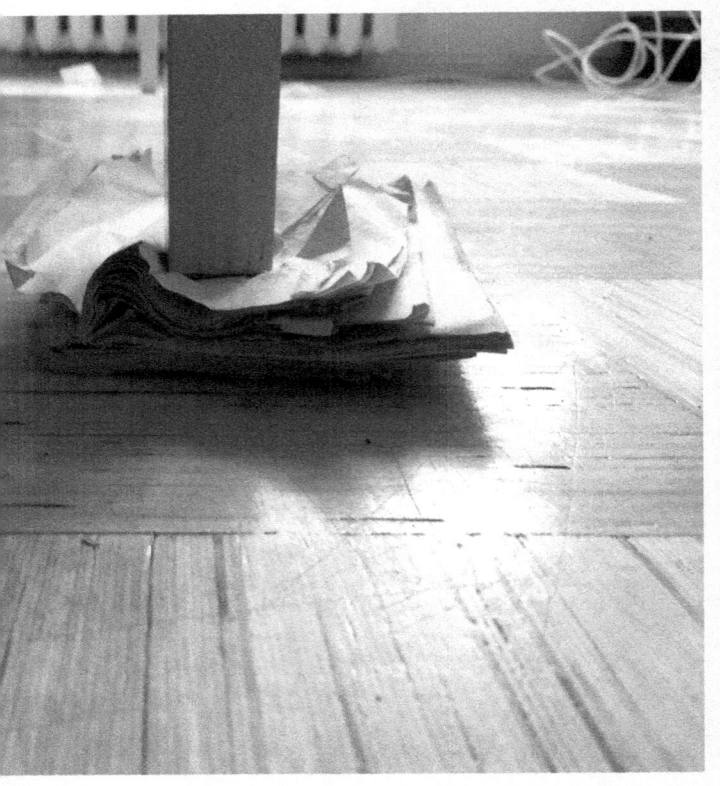

THE ACT OF BENDING A PAGE

129

ACT I

END OF ACT

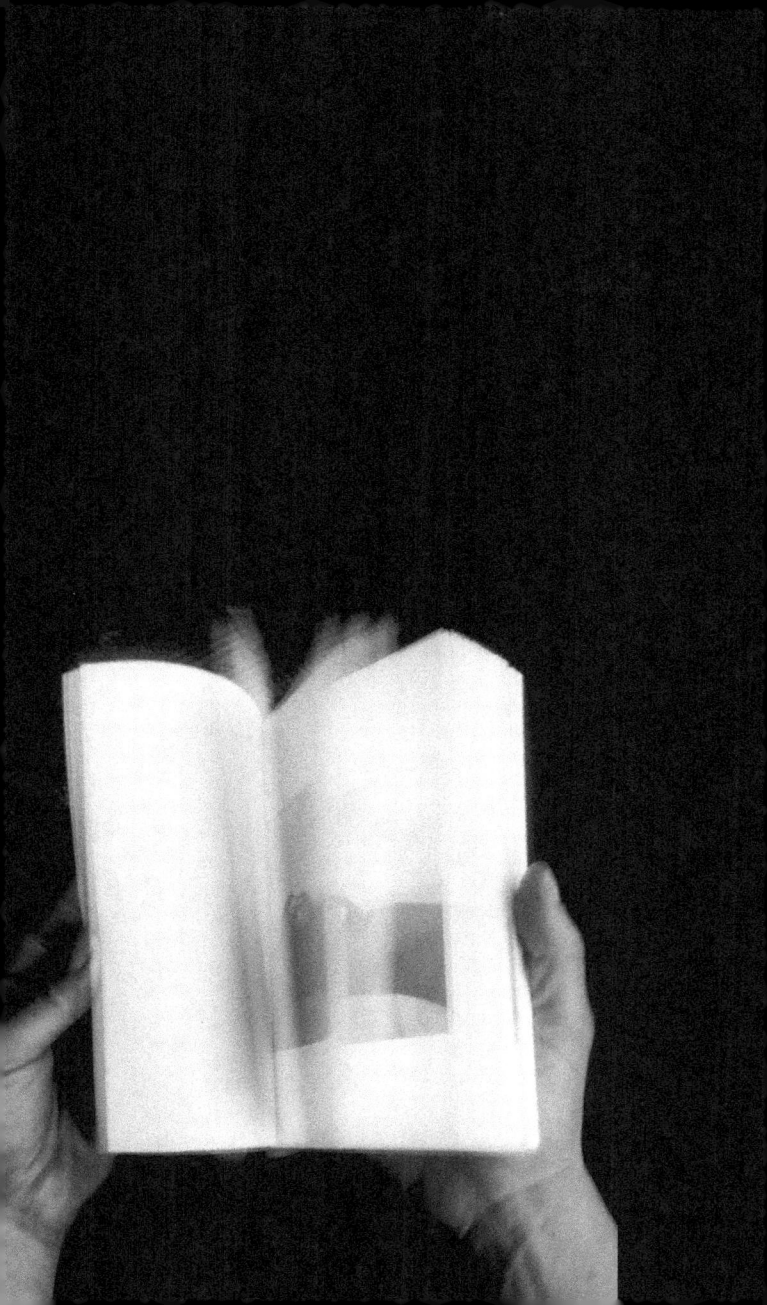

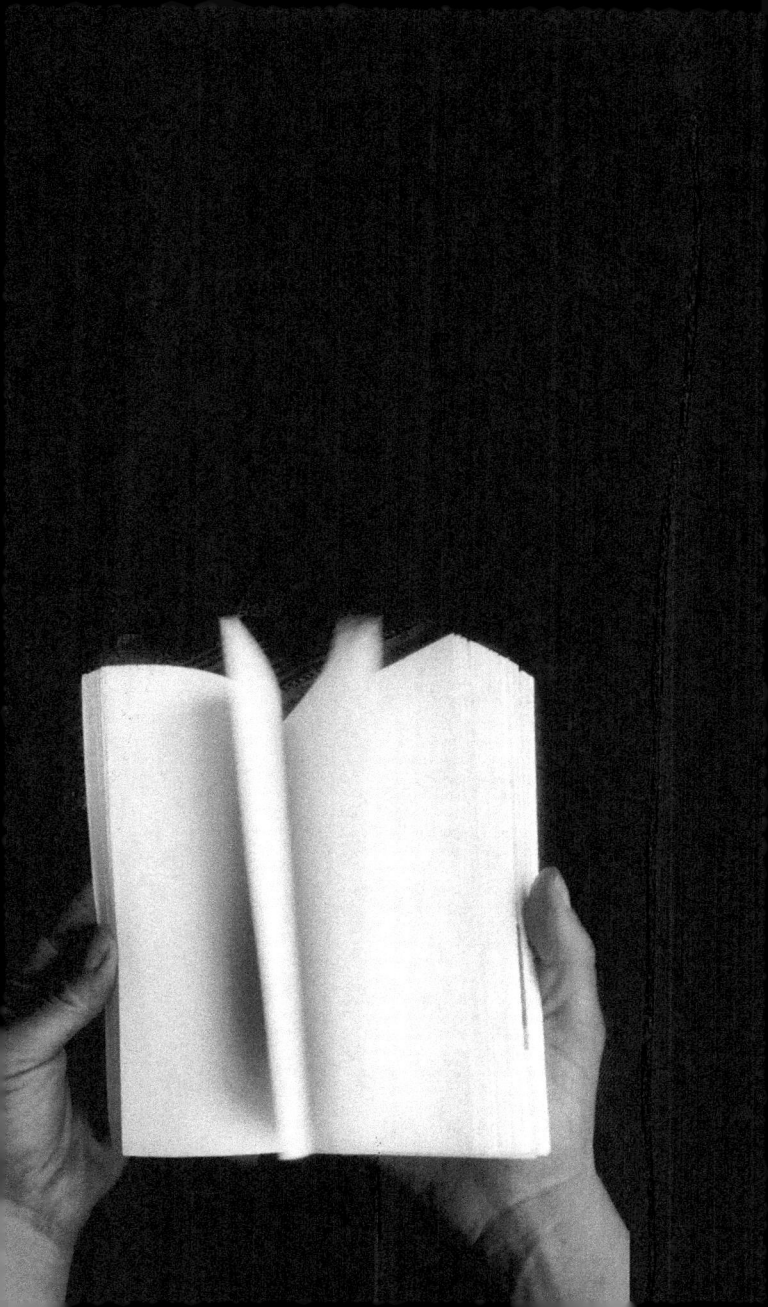

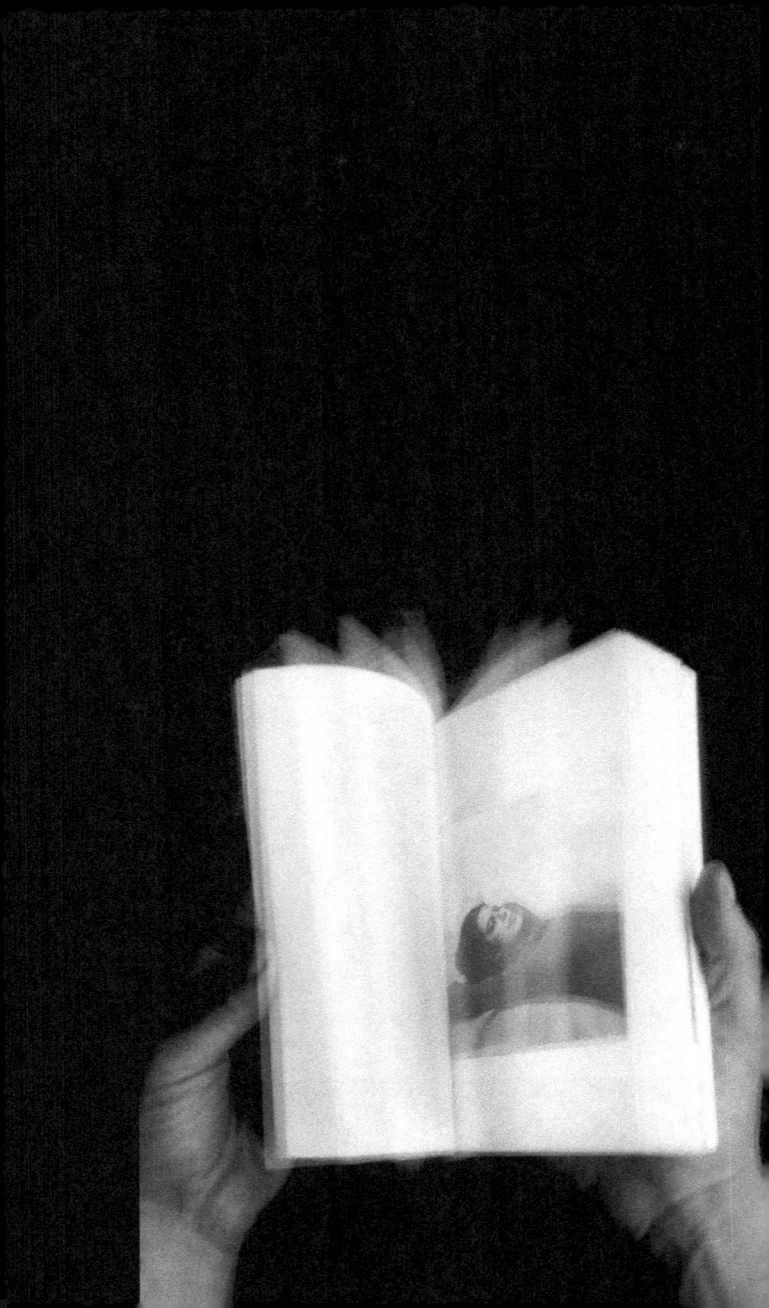

Shipment Summary

www.lulu.com
Lulu Enterprises
3101 Hillsborough St.
Raleigh, NC 27607
UNITED STATES

Received by:
Clara Lobregat Balaguer
668 QUIRINO AVENUE JALEVILLE S
52 SHORELINE STREET
PARAÑAQUE CITY METRO MANILA
PHILIPPINES
07762765095

Shipment Date: 28/05/2015
Shipped Via: DHL - MAIL MAIL
Order#: 10604371-1

Qty	Content ID	Description	Page Count
1	16717655	Blank Book 2·45 $	230

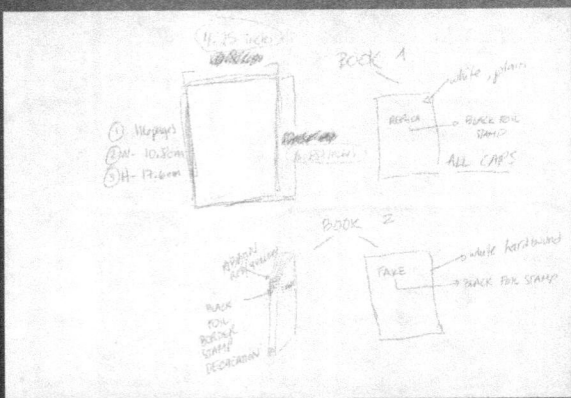

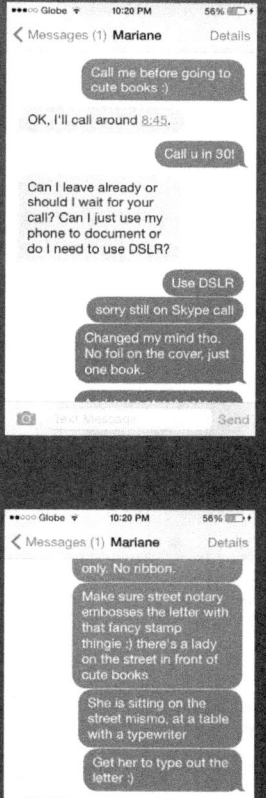

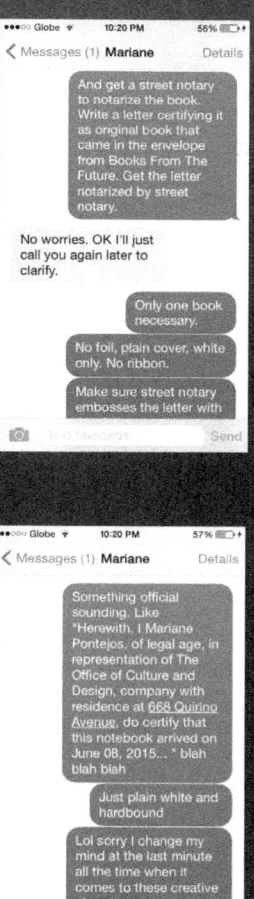

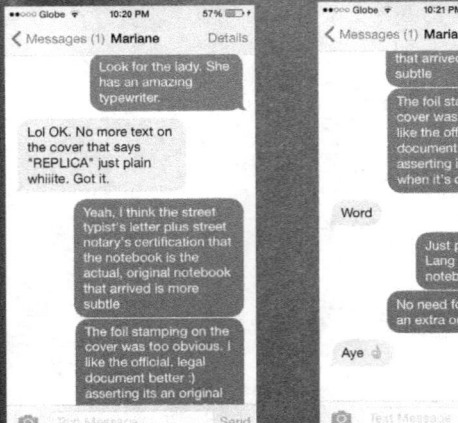

Screen 1 (10:20 PM):

> Look for the lady. She has an amazing typewriter.

Lol OK. No more text on the cover that says "REPLICA" just plain whiite. Got it.

> Yeah, I think the street typist's letter plus street notary's certification that the notebook is the actual, original notebook that arrived is more subtle

> The foil stamping on the cover was too obvious. I like the official, legal document better :) asserting its an original

Screen 2 (10:21 PM):

> that arrived is more subtle

> The foil stamping on the cover was too obvious. I like the official, legal document better :) asserting its an original when it's obviously fake

Word

> Just picture picture Lang ;) and just one notebook k?

> No need for spending on an extra one.

Aye

> #ahoy

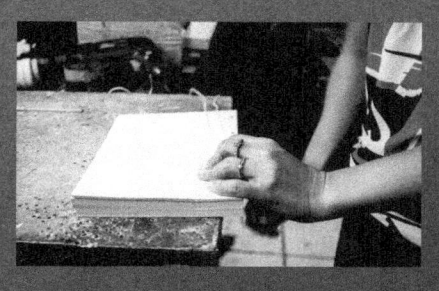

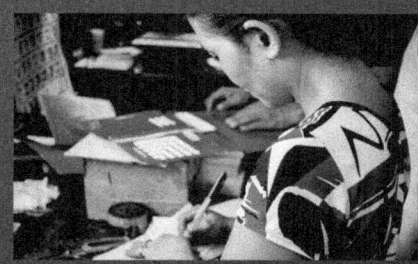

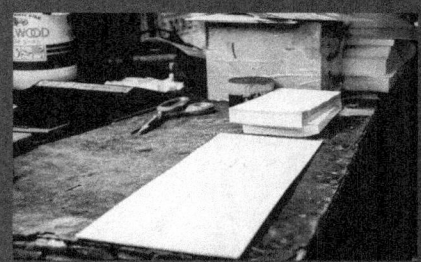

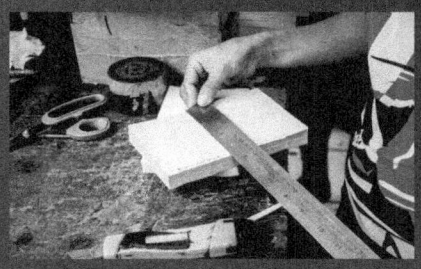

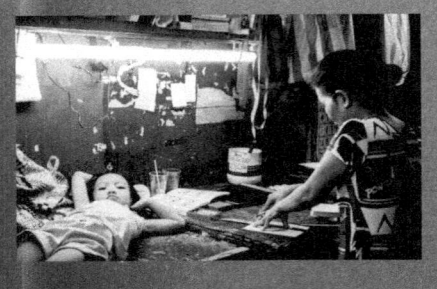

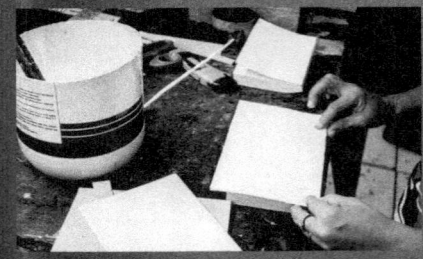

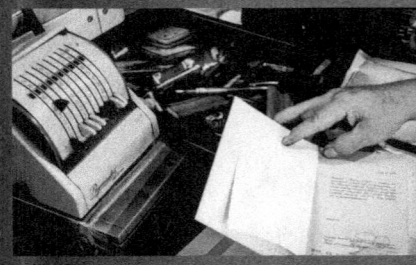

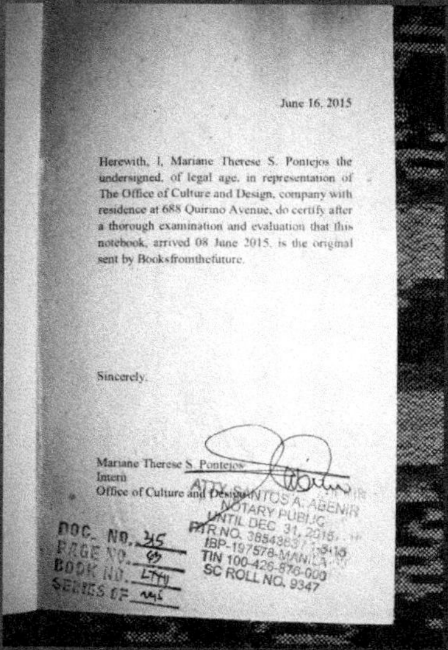

June 16, 2015

Herewith, I, Mariane Therese S. Pontejos the undersigned, of legal age, in representation of The Office of Culture and Design, company with residence at 688 Quirino Avenue, do certify after a thorough examination and evaluation that this notebook, arrived 08 June 2015, is the original sent by Booksfromthefuture.

Sincerely,

Mariane Therese S. Pontejos
Intern
Office of Culture and Design

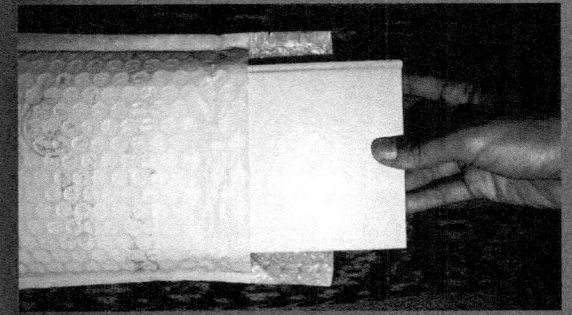

NOTARIZED FAKE ORIGINAL

In the Philippines, original copies of books are somewhat out of reach for the general public, pricewise, especially in the educational context. Textbooks, which account for the largest percentage of books published in the country, are expensive, so a booming and not-so-underground market for duplicating them exists, in many cases, sanctioned tacitly or openly by school administrations. Though primary and secondary school is free within the public school system, textbooks are not free. Public and private schools obligate families to buy books from the schools themselves, and these are often charged at a substantial mark-up that is prohibitive for low-income families. Schools use the sale of textbooks as an income source, as funding for educational institutions from the government is notoriously slim. Schools in rural areas often see students sharing textbooks, as precariously as one book to six students, if they are lucky to have any books at all, in smaller schools.

In the Philippines, originality is difficult, on many levels. We are taught from a very young age not to stand out, which would mean disharmony in the community. If one has an original idea that works, harmony is broken by envy of the pioneer's success and her relationships with community members are jeopardised. If one has an original idea that doesn't work, the pioneer is immediately singled out for punishment, ridicule or ostracism. There is nothing worse in the psyche of the Filipino than suffering dislocation from his community, so originality is

often eschewed for the sake of maintaining the warm succour of belonging to the group. Originality here can be dangerous to one's emotional health.

In the Philippines, over four centuries of colonial rule has muddled our sense of identity, our capability of independent and original thought. The long arm of postcolonial inferiority complex has instilled the idea that what is original to us, what is local or native, is of lesser value than what comes from other more developed countries. Coupled with our legendary prowess for mimicry, this provides a fertile breeding ground for the culture of counterfeiting to emerge.

In the Philippines, widespread corruption also abets the counterfeit culture. A fake university diploma, driver's license, seaman's book or passport may easily be acquired at roadside stalls in the downtown area of Metro Manila. Real notarisations of questionable documents are also easy to come by, and cost as much as the smallest bottle of distilled drinking water, or a medium-sized bottle of carbonated soda beverage.

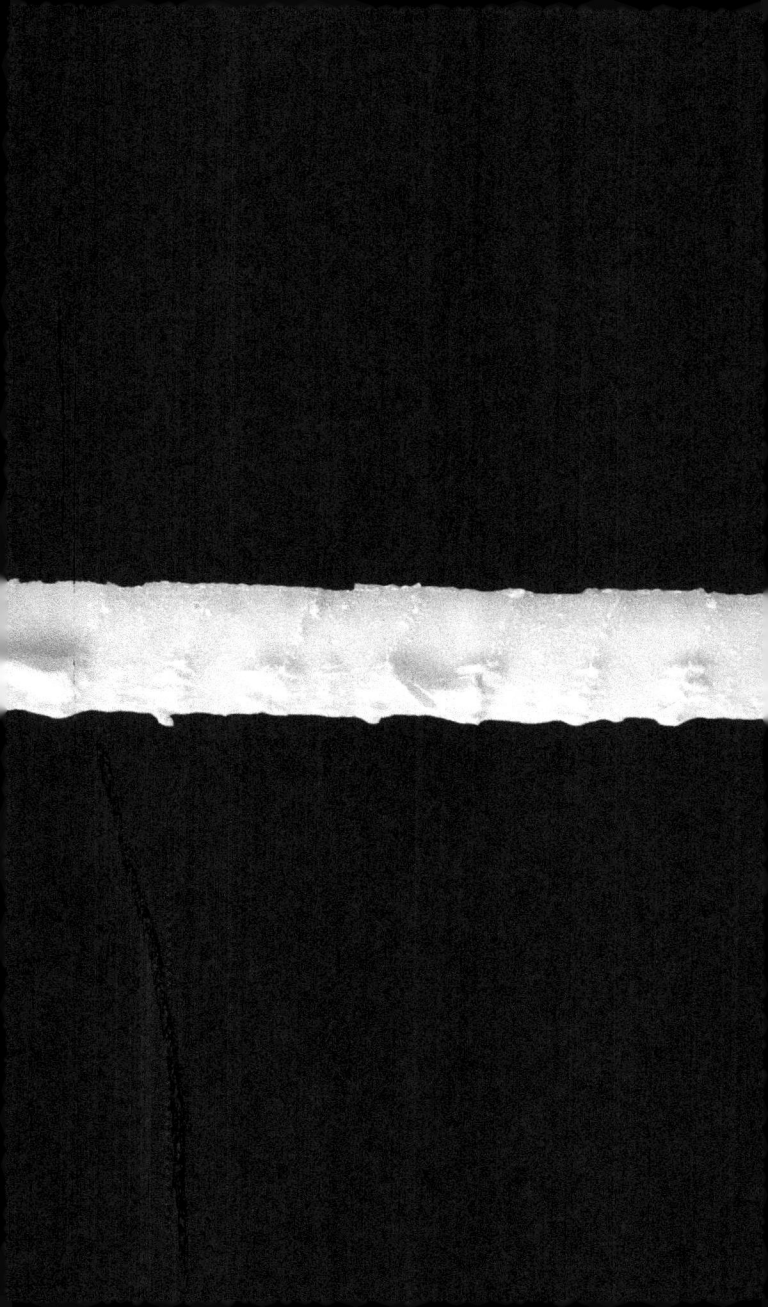

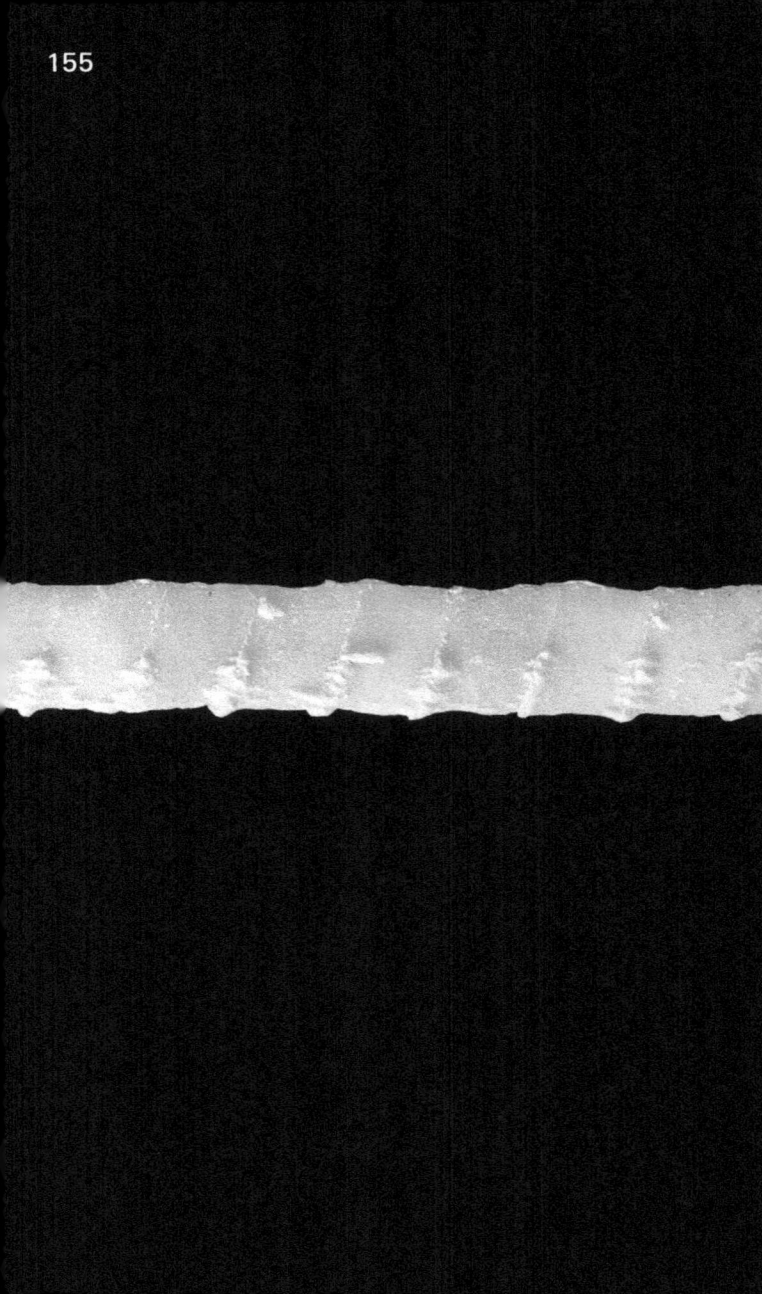

Choose a book from the shelf. With an eraser carefully coax total blankness from each page, working from bottom to top. Return the book to the shelf.

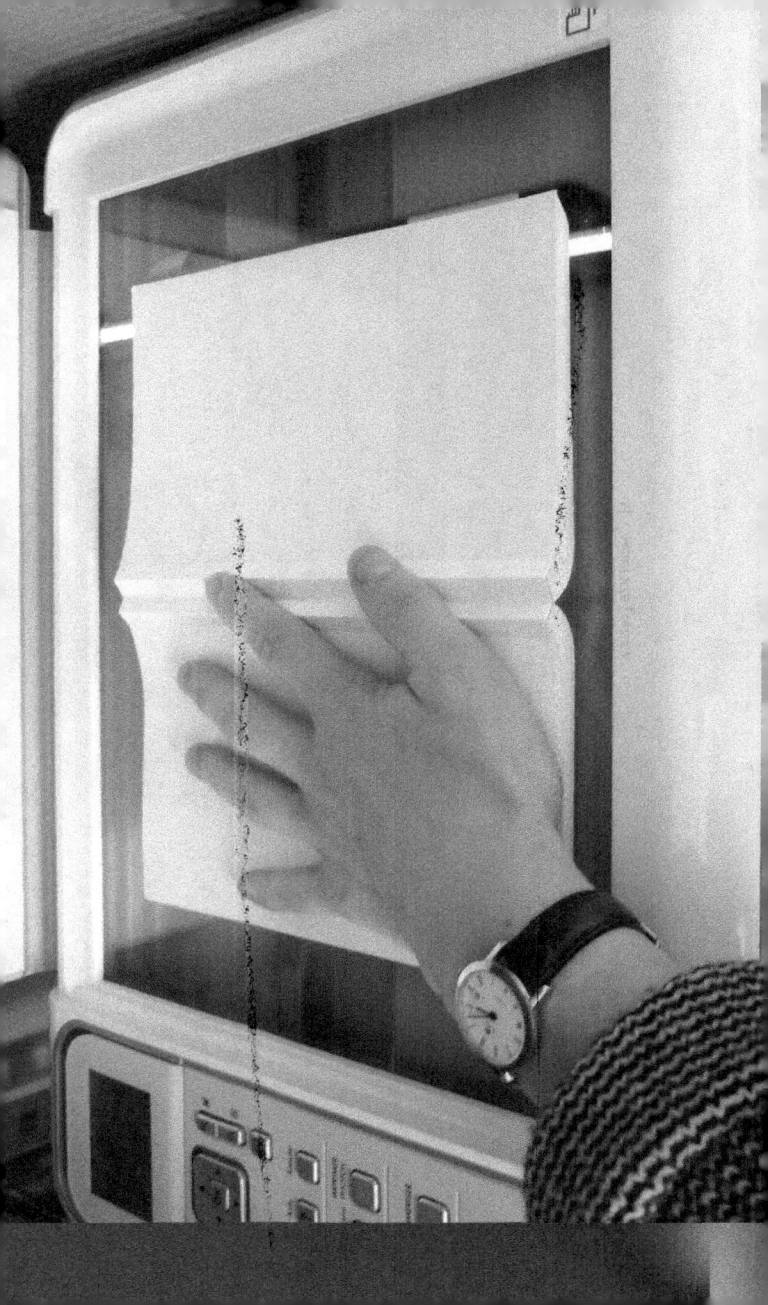

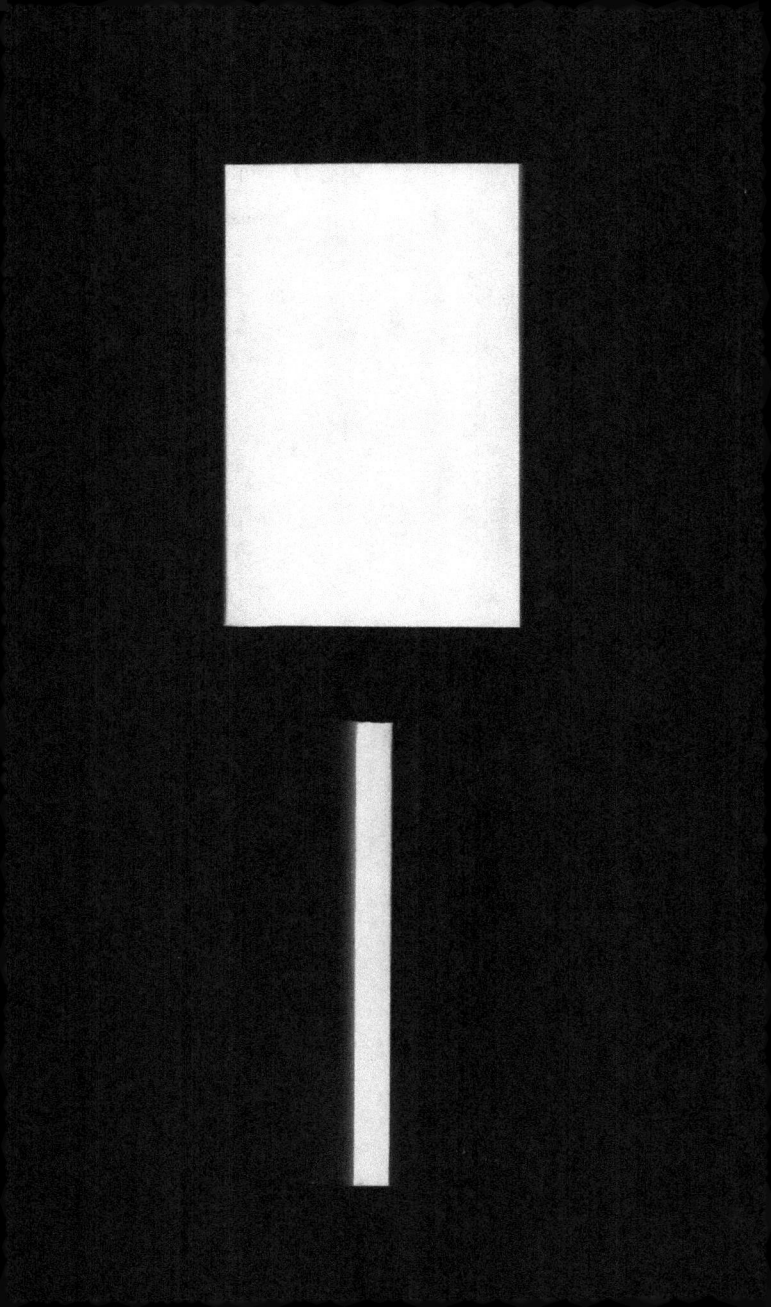

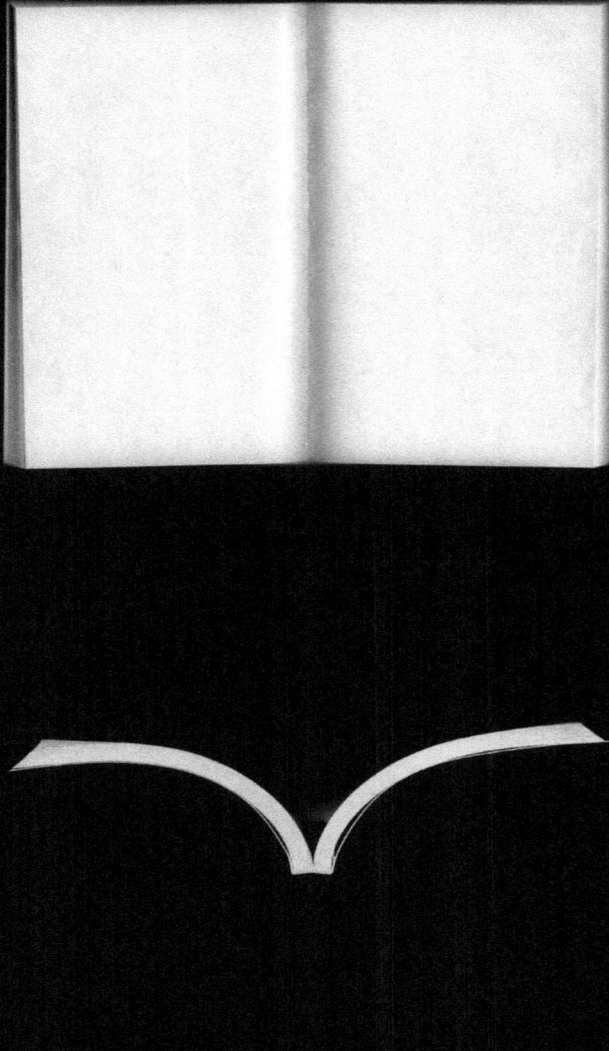

3121 MELBOURNE AU

G.D.A.A (Graphic Designer as Architect) was established in 2015. Born from Graphic Design's admiration towards Architecture's role of possessing socio-cultural status, historical significance and creating "works of art".

G.D.A.A aims to achieve equal or greater status for the Graphic Design discipline. This is attained by creating works incorporating architectural methodologies into graphic design practice – by following a site-specific manifesto.

From this manifesto, "Booq" was created.

Booq is a typeface consisting of interlocking components based on the architectural structure of the blank book provided by Booksfromthefuture. Booq is built upon a set of rules – only utilising the cover, spine, spread, arc and manipulating the paper of the book as the dimensional structure to construct a typeface.

By distributing the typeface to the participants in the workshop (for them to use and share, in or out of the workshop) the "documentation" in turn becomes a live performance.

SITE-SPECIFIC MANIFESTO
G.D.A.A

1
You must make a declaration by fulfilling
the blank spaces with words that compare or
reference Graphic Design and Architecture:

" _____ as _____ "

2
This manifesto declares "Book as Architecture"

3
Measure the book's dimensions of cover, spine,
spread, arch of the opened book[1] and folded angles
of the page[2]

4
The cover dimension is the main character width
and height

5
The spread dimension is the maximum character
width. Only used for symmetrical characters[3]

6
The spine is the stroke width

7
The arch of the opened book is the stroke arc

8
Create a typeface following the above rules

9
The typeface is to be shared under the Creative Commons license (Attribution-NoDerivatives 4.0 International)[4] provided to participants of Booksfromthefuture Summer School 2015

10
The typeface is to be used by participants both inside and outside the workshop, subsequently disseminating G.D.A.A's impetus in the digital realm

1 The arch is to be measured by placing the book on a flat surface, and opening it until the cover touches the flat surface. Measure the angle.

2 Fold the top and bottom corners of the page inwards to the spine. The crease mark on the page is your angle (45 degrees).

3 Symmetrical characters include case sensitive: A, H, I, M, O, T, U, V, W, X, Y, o, t, v, w, x.

4 You are free to copy and redistribute the material in any medium or format for any purpose, including commercially. You must give appropriate credit, provide a link to the license, and indicate if changes were made. You may do so in any reasonable manner, but not in any way that suggests the licensor endorses you or your use. If you remix, transform, or build upon the material, you may not distribute the modified material.

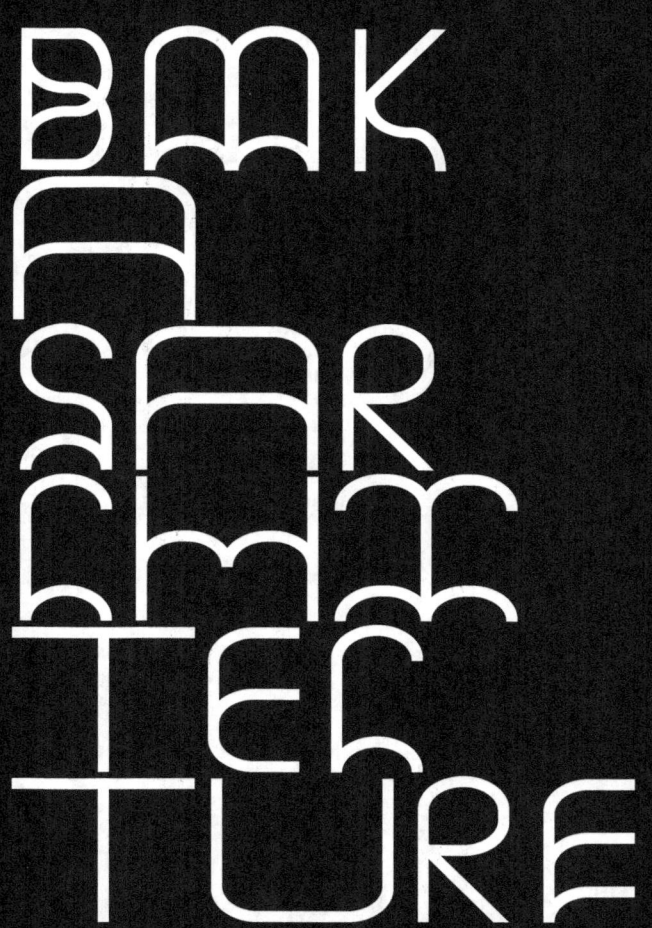

BMK ARCHITECTURE

Booq

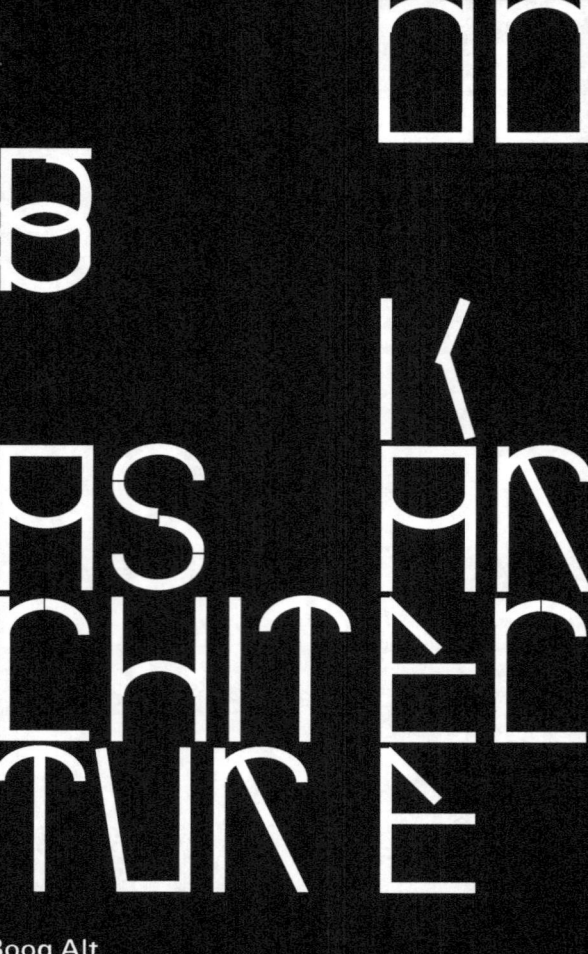

BOOKS AS AN ARCHITECTURE

loop
Screen
Book

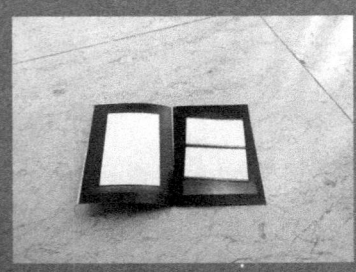

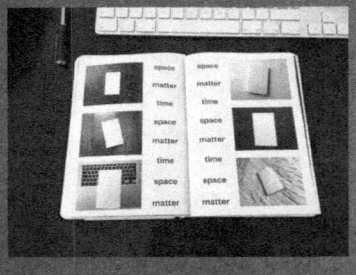

A Book

"The absences in a book create, one by one, a new book." "The absences in a book make the book never stop turning into a book".[1] Documenting the life of a blank book, by making another book.

The Infinite

The blank book is in itself a metaphor for absence, and a metaphor of infinite possibilities. If it is in this absence of books that we create another book, another thought, another idea, it's in a blank book that we experience total infinitude.

The Matter

A book is an object, it's matter, occupies a space. Has a weight, a measure. It can be touched, moved. The book is documented in different physical spaces.

A Scene

We move the book. We see it moving, we feel it, we film it. The book is a scene. A space for deambulation.

The Screen

Representing, documenting the book. Transposing this representation into another realm: a digital one. In the digital plan – the book dematerialises, but it stays an object.

A Machine

The book is a machine for new thoughts.
Another kind of infinitude presents. New narratives, a new context. An interaction of the many ideas of a blank book. The book online as a book and not its content.

A Loop

1 Edmond Jabès

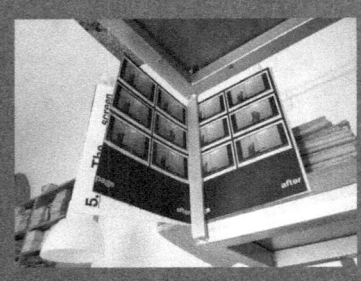

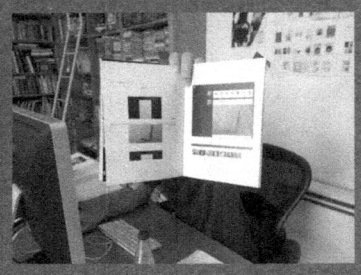

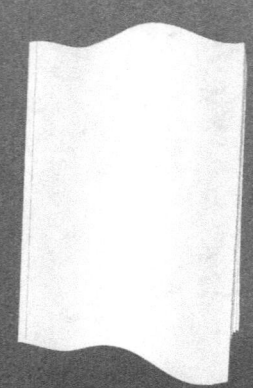

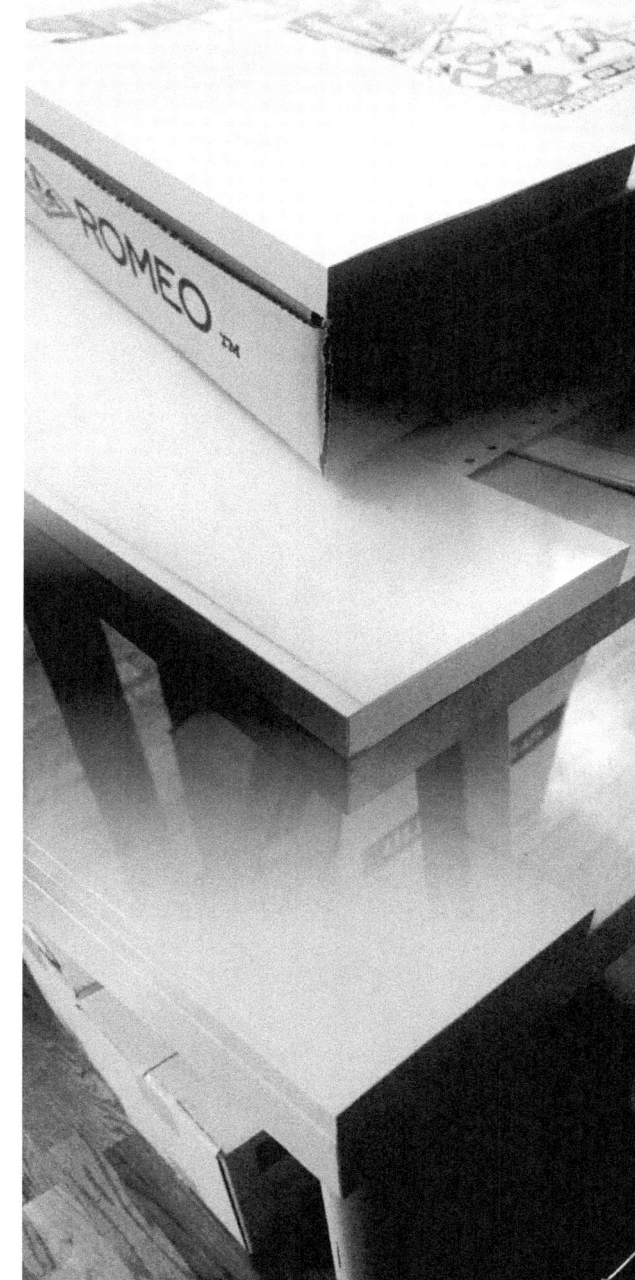

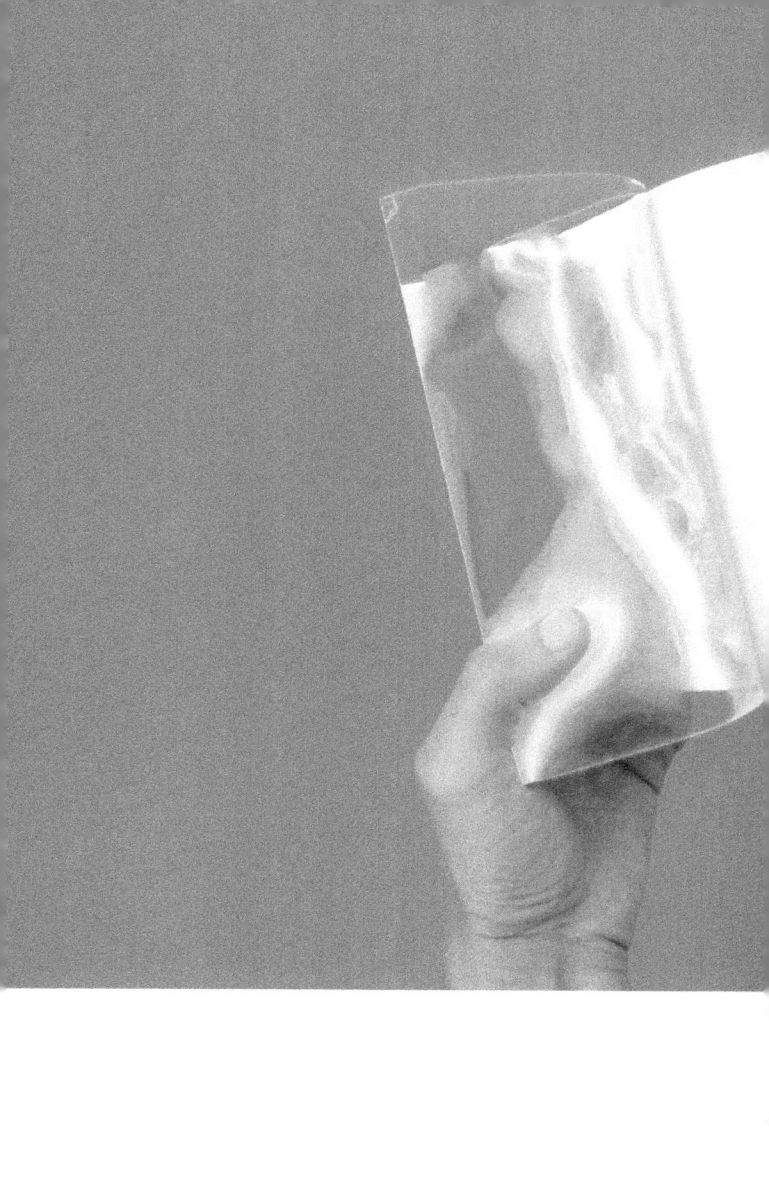

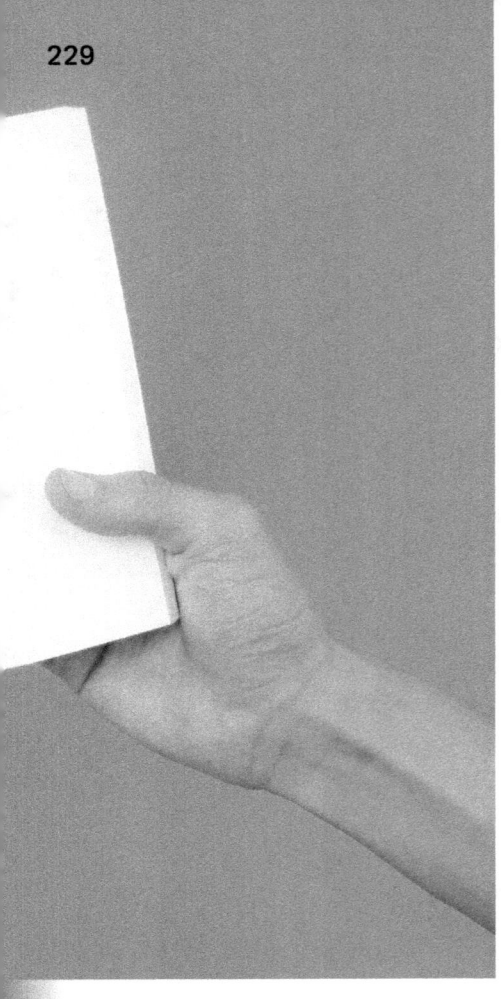

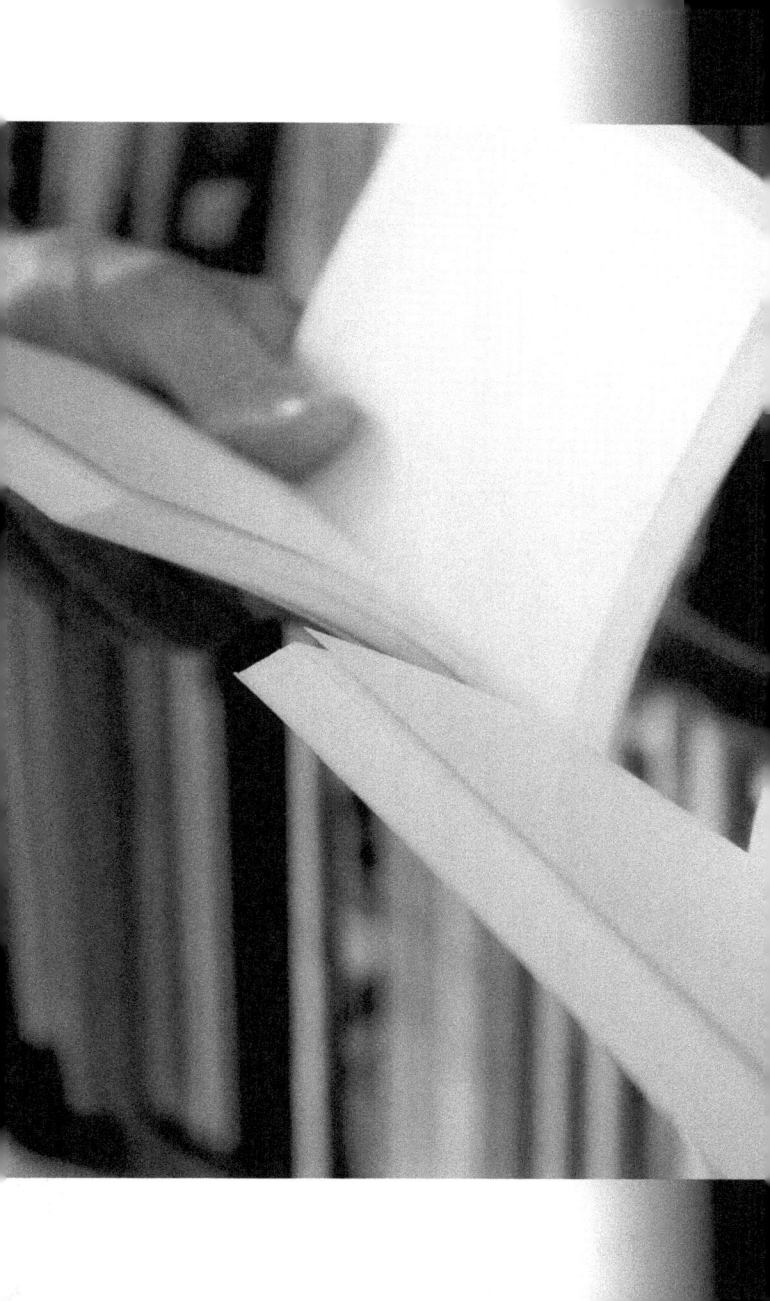

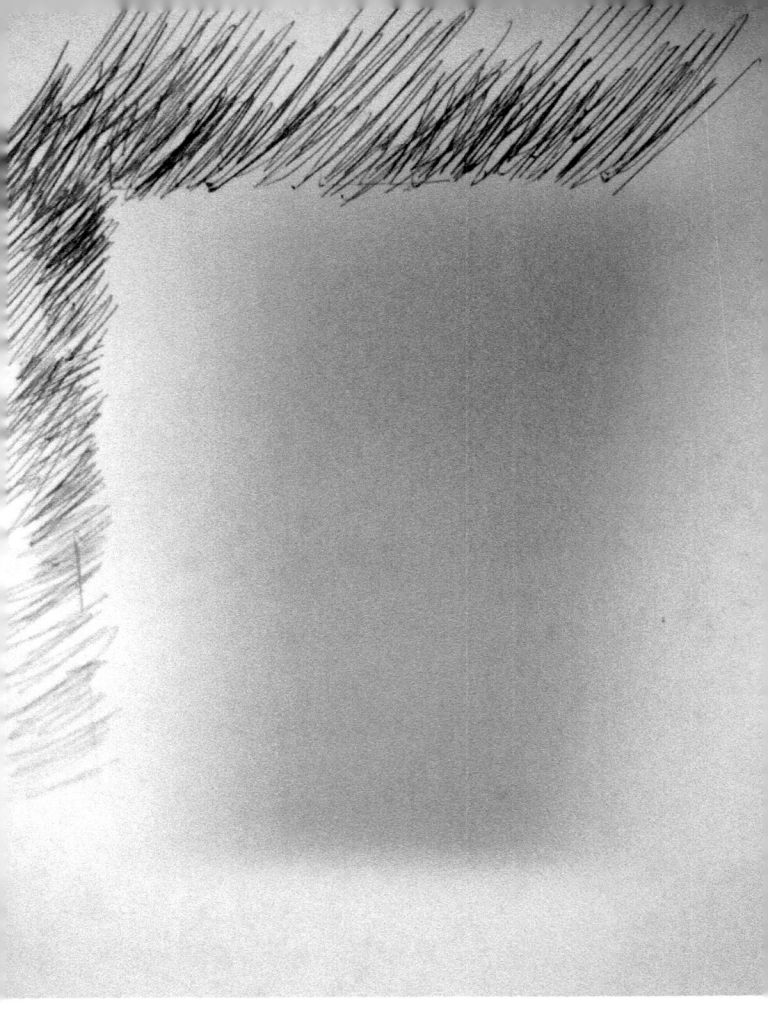

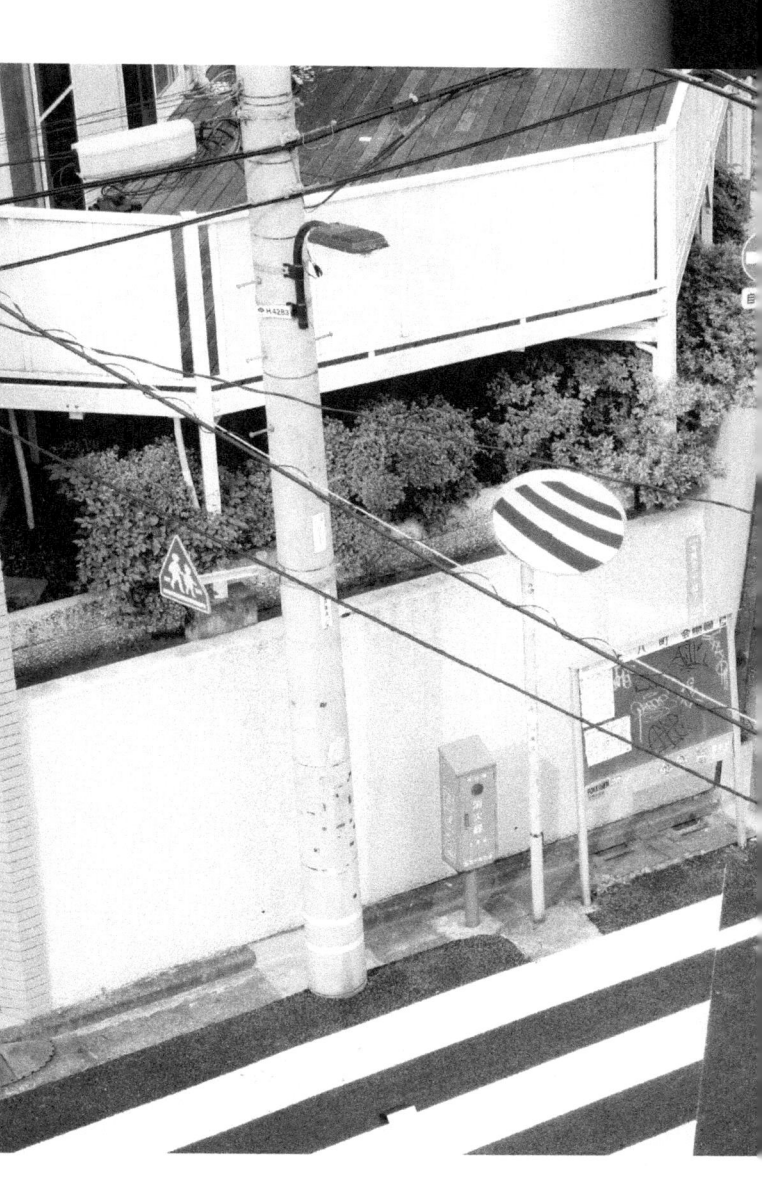

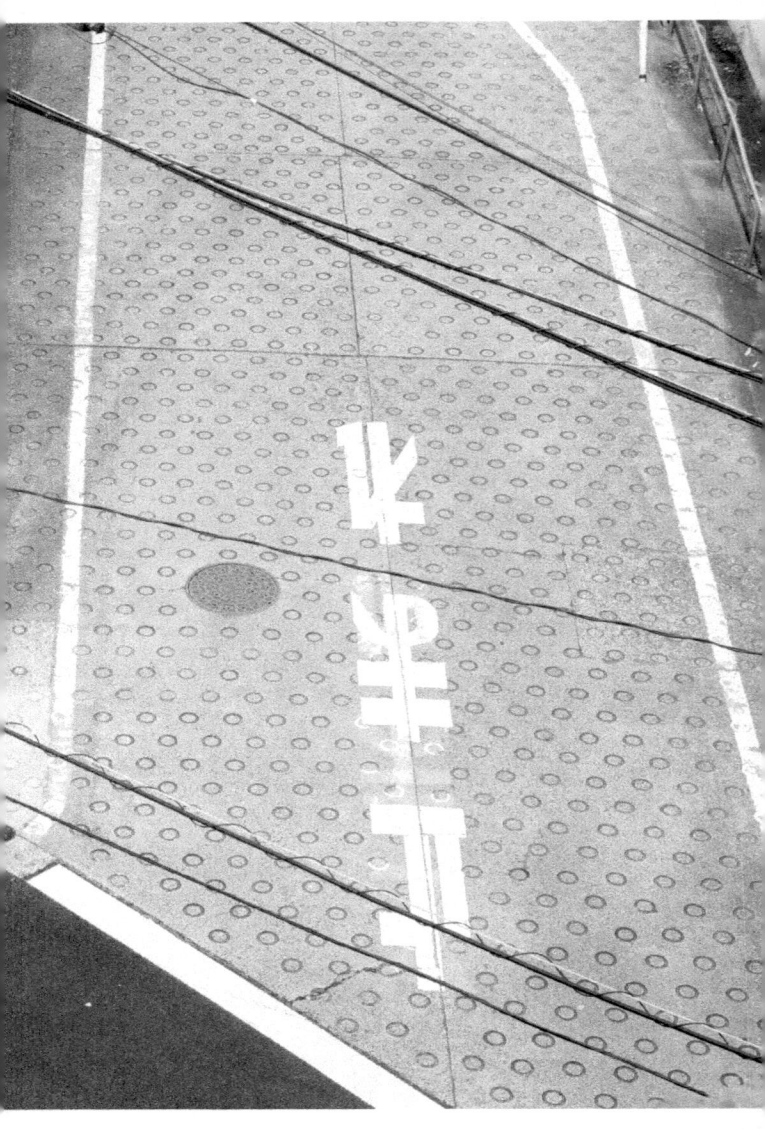

242

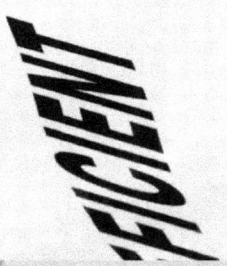

LES

PLINE

FICIENT

91600 SAVIGNY SUR ORGE FR

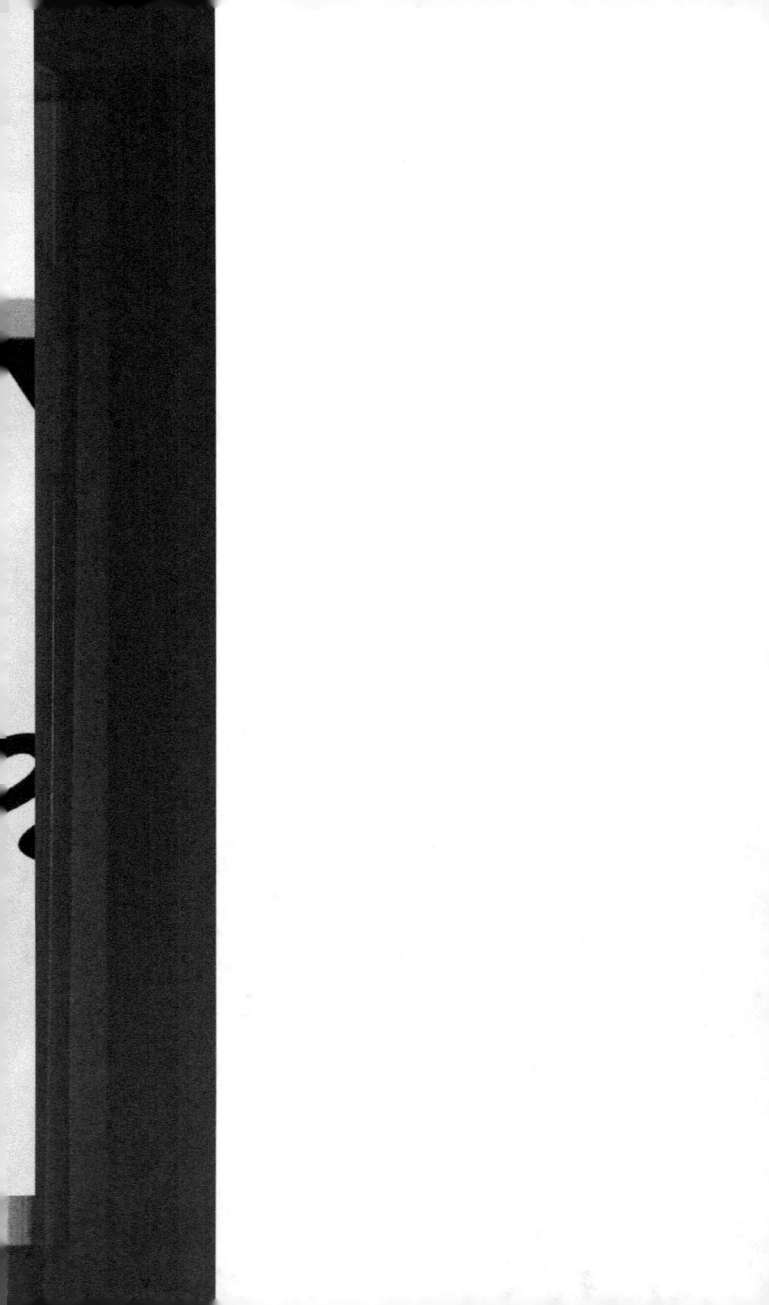

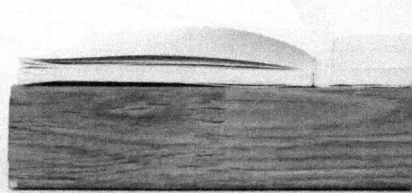

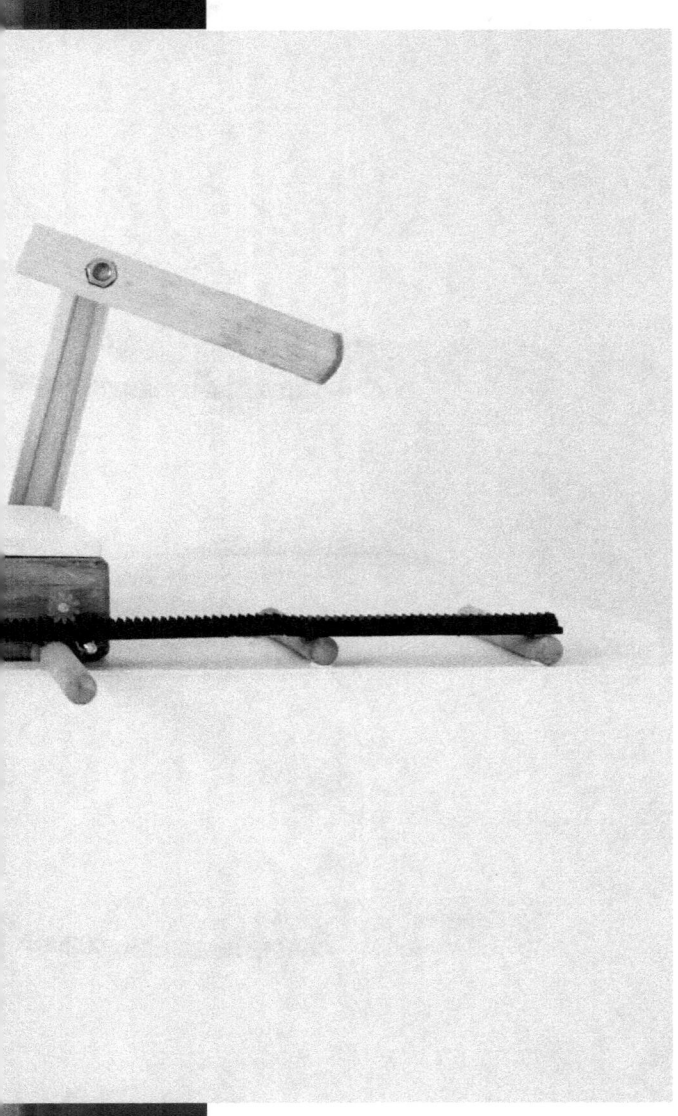

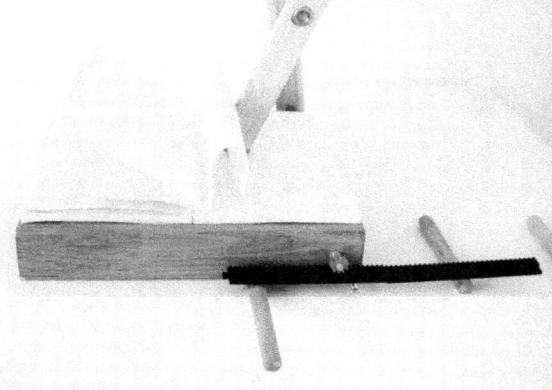

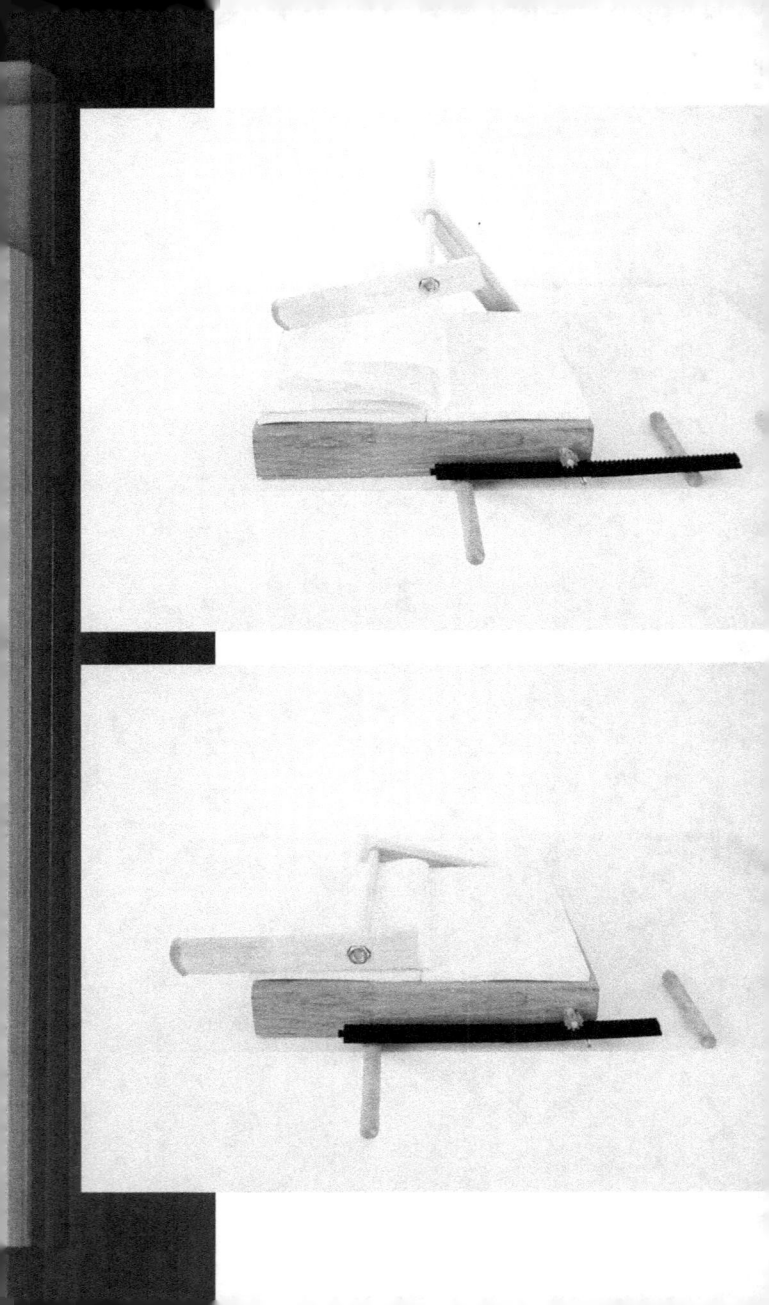

EVERYBODY'S BOOK OF ACTING CHARADES
(1897–2015)

Photocopy the following sequence of strips.

Cut each strip to size.

Position the strips throughout the pages of a blank book, one strip per page. Each strip's left edge should be as close as possible to the spine.

Close the book and wrap a rubber band around it, parallel to the spine, to keep the strips in place.

Open the book at a random page and read aloud the found strip.

Repeat until unamused, letting chance direct your performance.

Small hall; if possible, hung with banners, devices, etc.

[*Enter* LANDLADY.]

Landlady. A letter for you, Sir.

[*Another knock. Enter* PICTURE DEALER, *excitedly.*]

Costumes.

Not too modern; but *quite* appropriate for each character.

Chairman. Ladies and gentlemen, the subject for discussion this evening, is "What to Do with Our Sons." (Hear,

Editor. May I ask for the title?

[HARRY *gets up and looks out of window.*]

Third Visitor. [*Interrupting.*] Of *course* it is original.

Harry. Well, Angelina, is dinner ready? It is one o'clock. [*Takes out his watch.*]

Harry. [*Solo.*] Dear me! I *do* like punctuality. [*Pause.*]

[*Enter* LANDLADY—*right.*]

Aunt. Oh, you heartless, cruel fellow! [*To nephew.*]

(*Hear, hear and applause.*)

Old Gentleman. She will honour us with her company, I hope. Madam, you will, I trust, join our little party.

[*Enter* JOHN *hastily and excited.*]

Mr. Brag. Oh, but you *must* come. It'll be *so* jolly. Now be sociable and friendly.

[*Enter* TRAVELLER *at right.*]

[SCENE.—*as before. Enter* ARTIST.]

[ANGELINA *goes to window.*]

Joker. [*Very slowly and emphatically.*] You each received a letter, did you not?

Artist. [*Going forward.*] I am that individual.

[*After a slight pause the conversation is continued.*]

[*Artist Laughs. Enter noisily* MR. BRAG, *friend of Artist. Exit* LANDLADY.]

Old Gentleman. That's well. I propose a visit to the Crystal Palace. Are you all agreeable to this?

Artist. Y—e—es! [*Slowly.*]

Harry. [*Trying to look cheerful.*] What's that?

BUTLER.   Appropriate dress.

Editor. [*Eagerly.*] Stop! stop! *that's* not original

Loveman. And since you have broken silence, I may as well return the compliment—your conduct to me is simply doubly unparalleled! And if——

Sweetman. [*Interrupting.*] And if there were any ground or cause for your remarkable, your unaccountable behaviour, I could understand it. I begin to question your perfect sanity.

Artist. Yes, I must confess this is good news—but.

ACT I.

[SCENE.—*Artist's Studio. Artist discovered, appropriately dressed, and seated at easel, painting, or walking about the room with hands in his pockets, soliloquizing.*]

(*A show of hands results in a majority for the motion.*)

Joker. I am glad to have met you, Madam. [*Bowing.*]

Editor. I hope it is original, as I——

(PAUSE.)

Play my part, and disappear.
[*Exit reluctantly.*]

Landlady. What does all this mean? Can't you explain?

[*Drawing-room.* LADY *seated working. Enter* GENTLEMAN *of house.*]

Landlady. Why, John, whatever *is* the matter? You want to leave?

Butler. [*After a pause.*] I hope, Ladies and Gentlemen, you do not forget the lateness of the hour, and need reminding it is quite time to retire.

ACT I.

[SCENE.—*Modern sitting-room. Young wife and visitor seated.*]

Sweetman. Oh, how nice. Let us read a little in this book, till they come; shall we? [*Sit quite close to each other and read. After a pause they look fixedly into each other's face.*] What a calm, placid face you have, Ebby!

Loveman. Oh, yes, my dear friend, I am so glad you have suggested it. I should like it immensely.

Mary. [*Very much confused, and not looking at him.*] Well! What is it? [*Seats herself in a chair, and fixes her eyes on the floor.*]

Artist. I—I—this is so sudden! You have taken me quite—

[*A knock is heard. Enter* OLD FRIEND *of* ARTIST'S.]

Artist. You must know I have been very short of money lately.

Loveman. I cannot acknowledge that! It is only your kindness to say so. [*Continues to read.*]

[*John waits a little, but is just about to leave, when*

ACT II.

(SCENE *as before,* LANDLADY *discovered seated in chair.*)

[*Enter* JOHN *bringing in* TRAVELLER'S *portmanteau.*]

Jane. [*Outside.*] This way, Sir, if you please, this way.

[*Enter* LANDLADY *with a letter.*]

Mary. [*Looking at them.*] Oh! John.

Angelina. [*Trying to appear cheerful.*] Do you think so?

John. Yes, Sir. [*Exit.*

I'll run away. [*Paces the room and gets quite excited.*]

All. Well, you certainly have been acting very strangely!

Angelina. Why, what *is* the matter with you, Uncle?

John. Beg pardon, Sir, this is your trunk I believe?

Uncle George. Were you laughing at me, Sir? and pray what for?

[*Pauses and goes to window.*] There now; it rains!

Uncle George. Ah! I'll set matters right. You have a little nap, now, and I'll go and find them.   [*Exit.*

[*A knock at the door is heard.*]

Aunt. [*Sharply.*] Did you address me, Sir?

Sweetman. Really, Mr. Vinegar, your words are enough to rouse the anger of a saint. [*Very loudly.*] You will provoke me, beyond the point of endurance.

Old Lady. You wicked fellow!

Aunt. Really, this is very pleasing and satisfactory.

[*A knock is heard. Enter* MR. JOKER, *a fellow clerk.*]

Loveman. [*Cooler, but provokingly.*] I'm not deaf, Mr. Sugar.

[*The two friends look at each other confusedly. After a pause.*]

Old Lady. I am afraid they have had a slight misunderstanding about something!

Old Gentleman. Well, young gentlemen, make yourselves ready, and we will start at once.

Small company of friends seated in dimly-lighted room.

Uncle George. Well, how about our little plan? Have you anything fresh to tell me? Do they get on together any better?

ACT I.

[SCENE.—*Sitting-room. Two friends—clerks, discovered seated at table, reading.*]

Room in country cottage. Village gossips talking together.

Artist. [*After reading letter.*] Merciful Goodness!

(CURTAIN.)

[*Covers her face and begins to cry again.*] There I am again!

Lady. But you haven't told me yet what's the matter!—

Harry. Is it not ready, then?

Rose. Now don't be foolish, Charlie.

Harry. [*Piqued.*] Well, I want a walk, and you don't like me to go out alone.

Traveller. Oh, 'tis a long story; and I would fain keep it from you.

[*A knock at the door is heard.*]

Aunt. [*Sharply.*] Did you address me, Sir?

Sweetman. Really, Mr. Vinegar, your words are enough to rouse the anger of a saint. [*Very loudly.*] You will provoke me, beyond the point of endurance.

Old Lady. You wicked fellow!

Aunt. Really, this is very pleasing and satisfactory.

[*A knock is heard. Enter* MR. JOKER, *a fellow clerk.*]

Loveman. [*Cooler, but provokingly.*] I'm not deaf, Mr. Sugar.

[*The two friends look at each other confusedly. After a pause.*]

Old Lady. I am afraid they have had a slight misunderstanding about something!

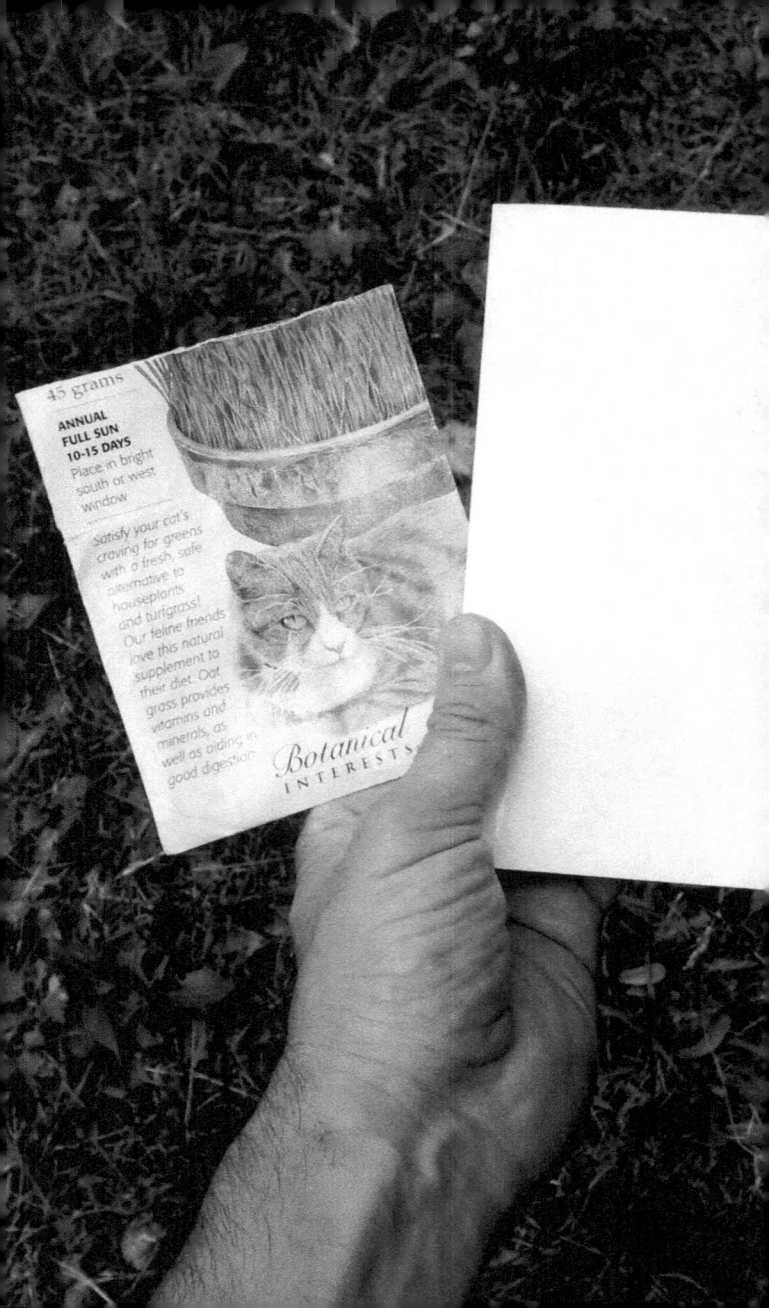

45 grams

**ANNUAL
FULL SUN
10-15 DAYS**
Place in bright
south or west
window

Satisfy your cat's
craving for greens
with a fresh, safe
alternative to
houseplants
and turfgrass!
Our feline friends
love this natural
supplement to
their diet. Oat
grass provides
vitamins and
minerals, as
well as aiding in
good digestion.

Botanical
INTERESTS

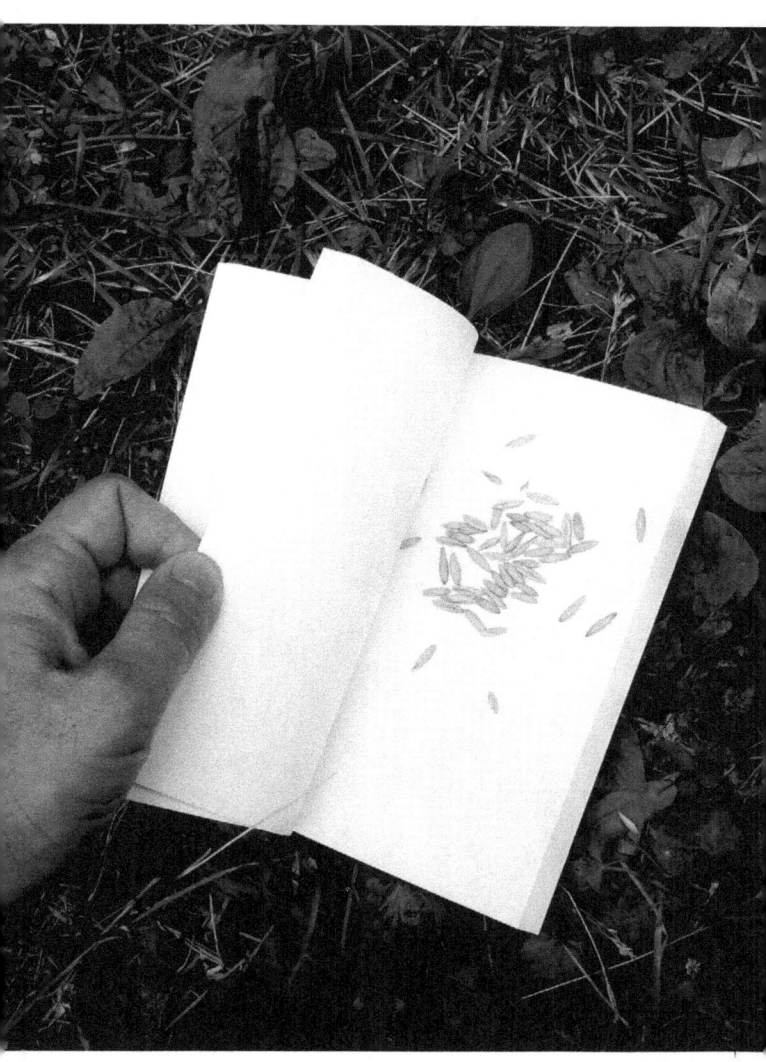

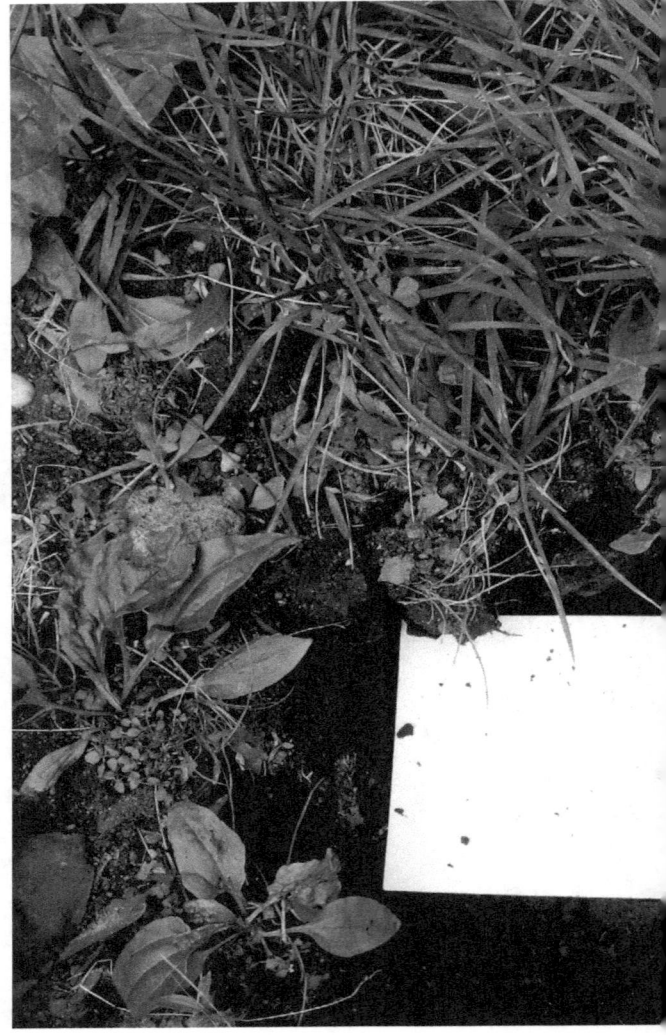

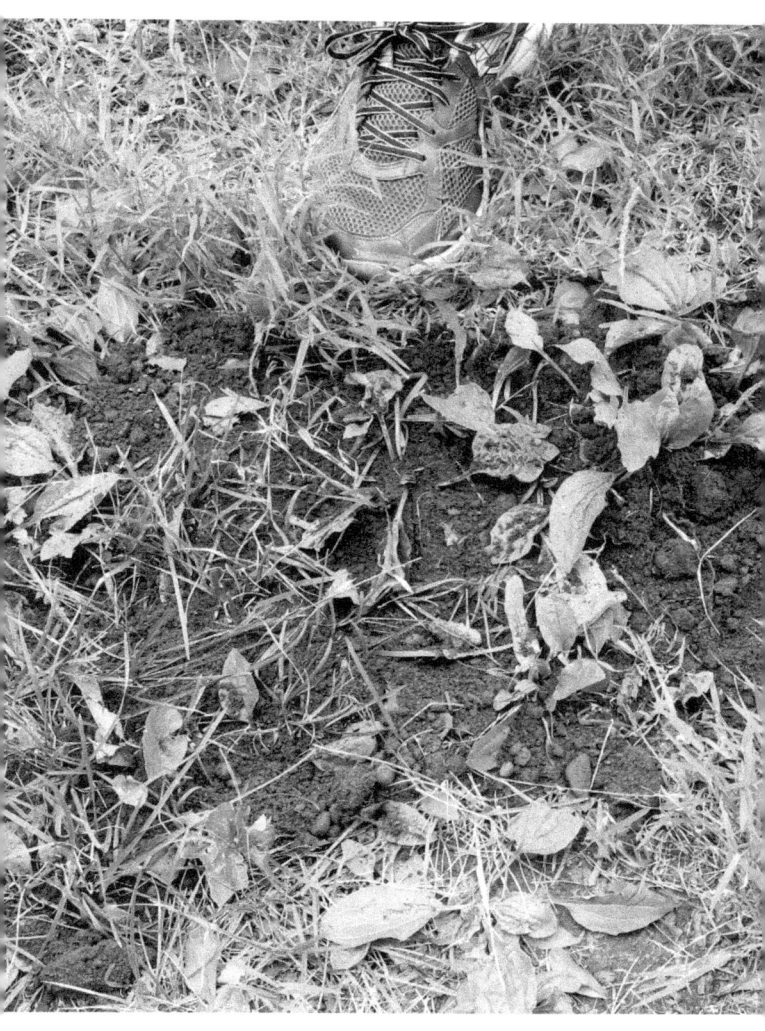

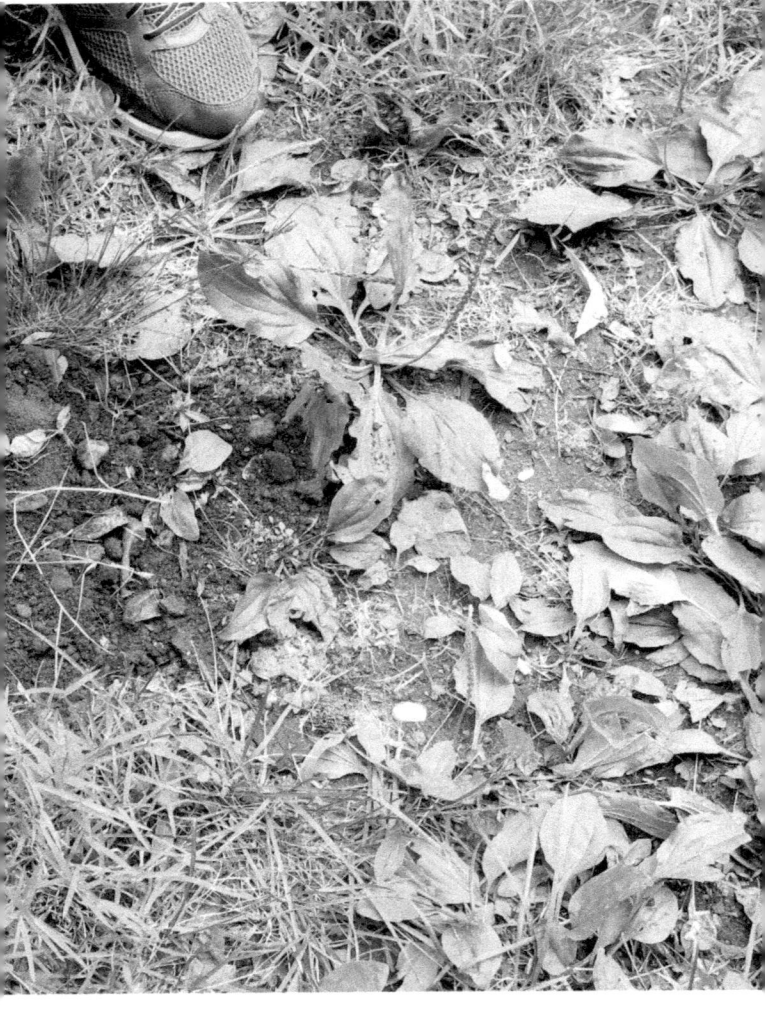

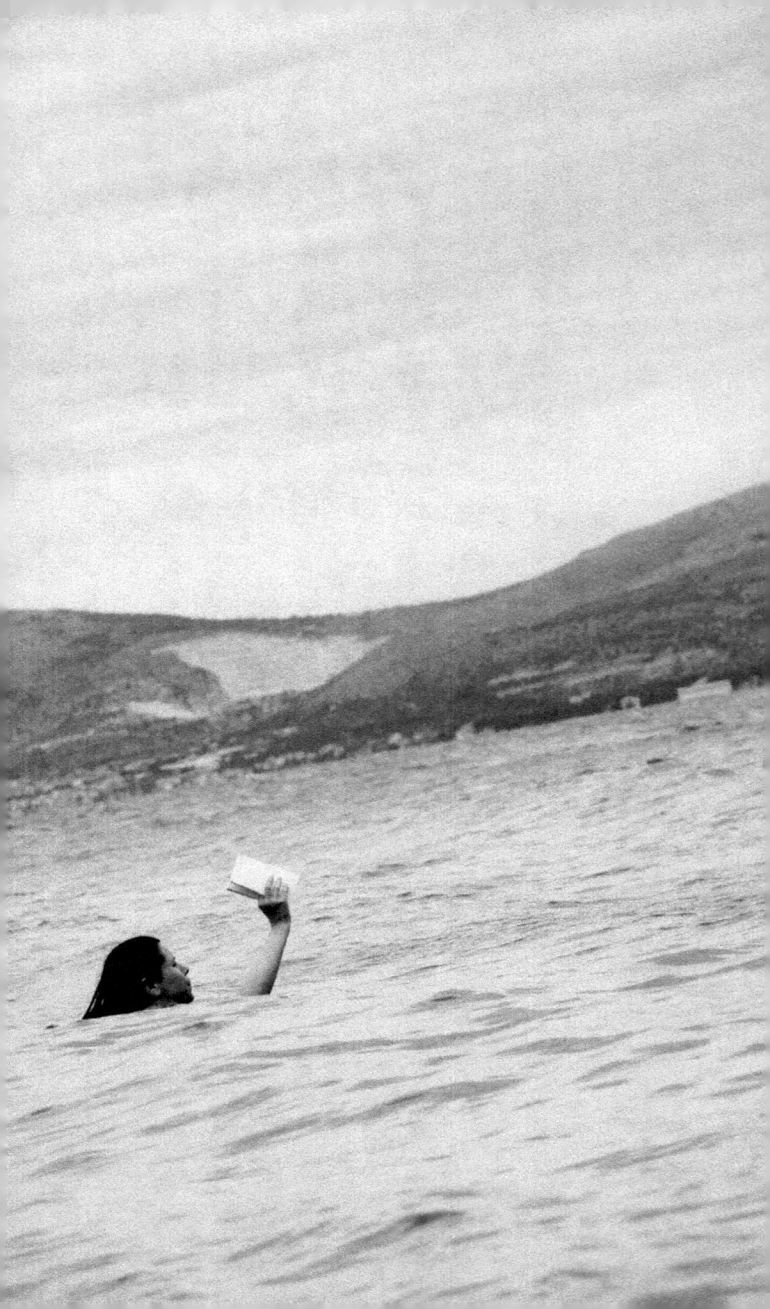

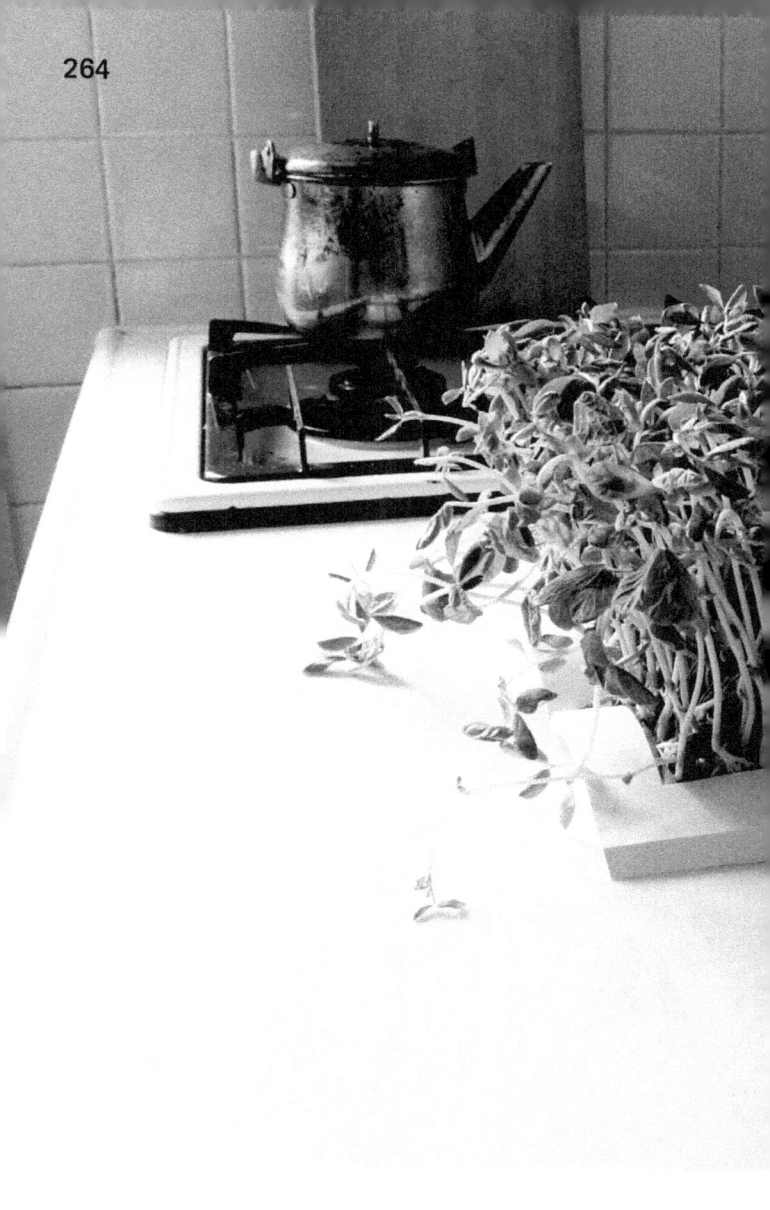

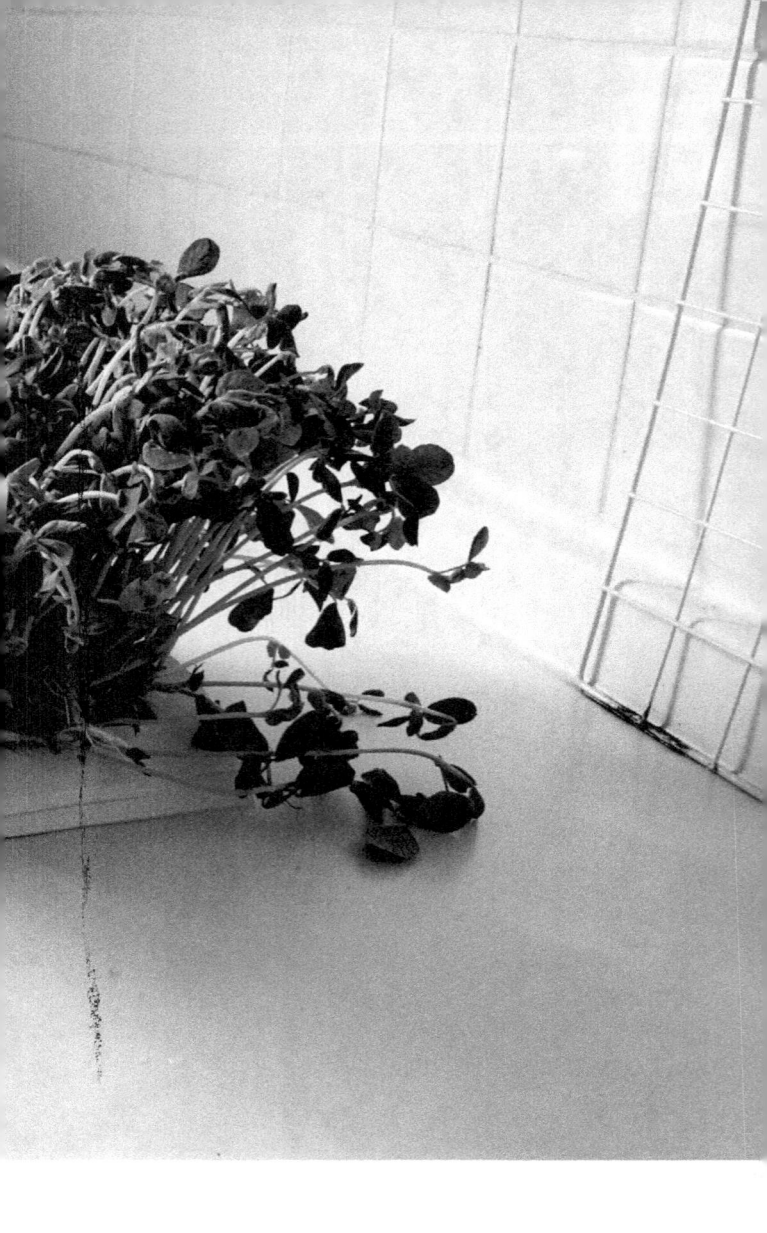

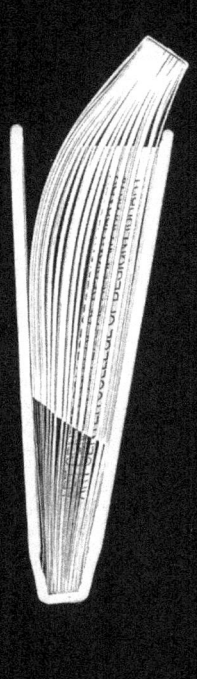

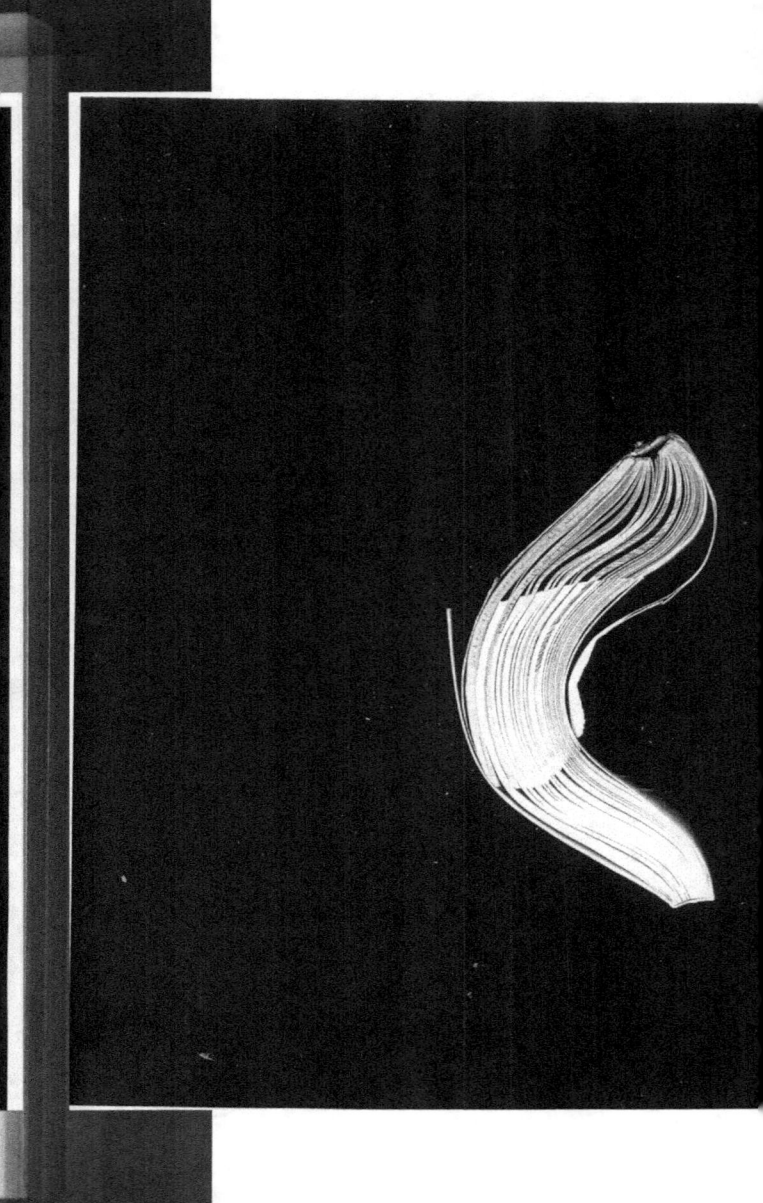

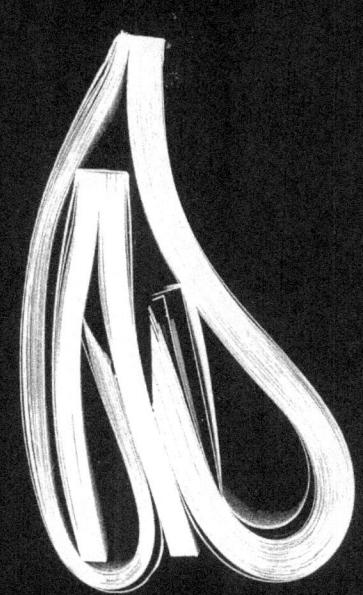

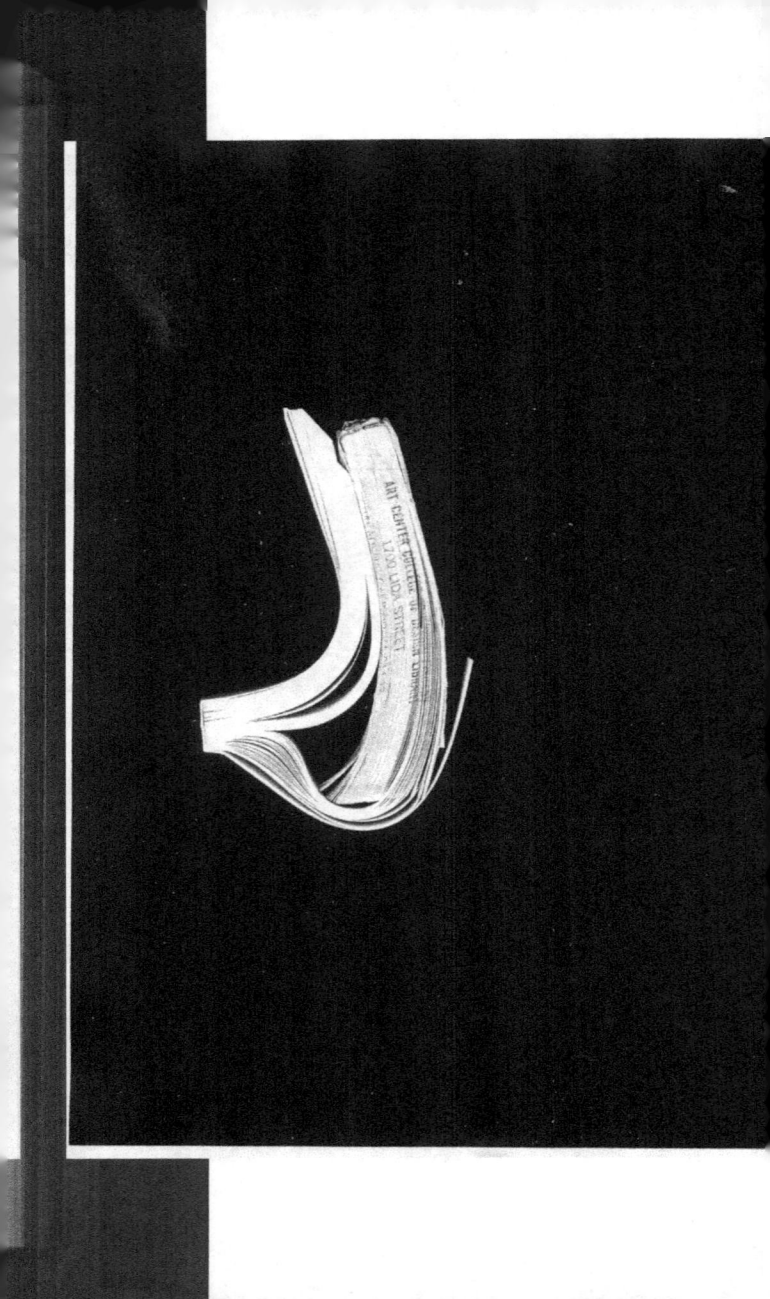

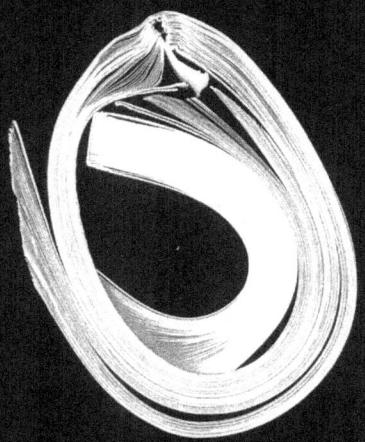

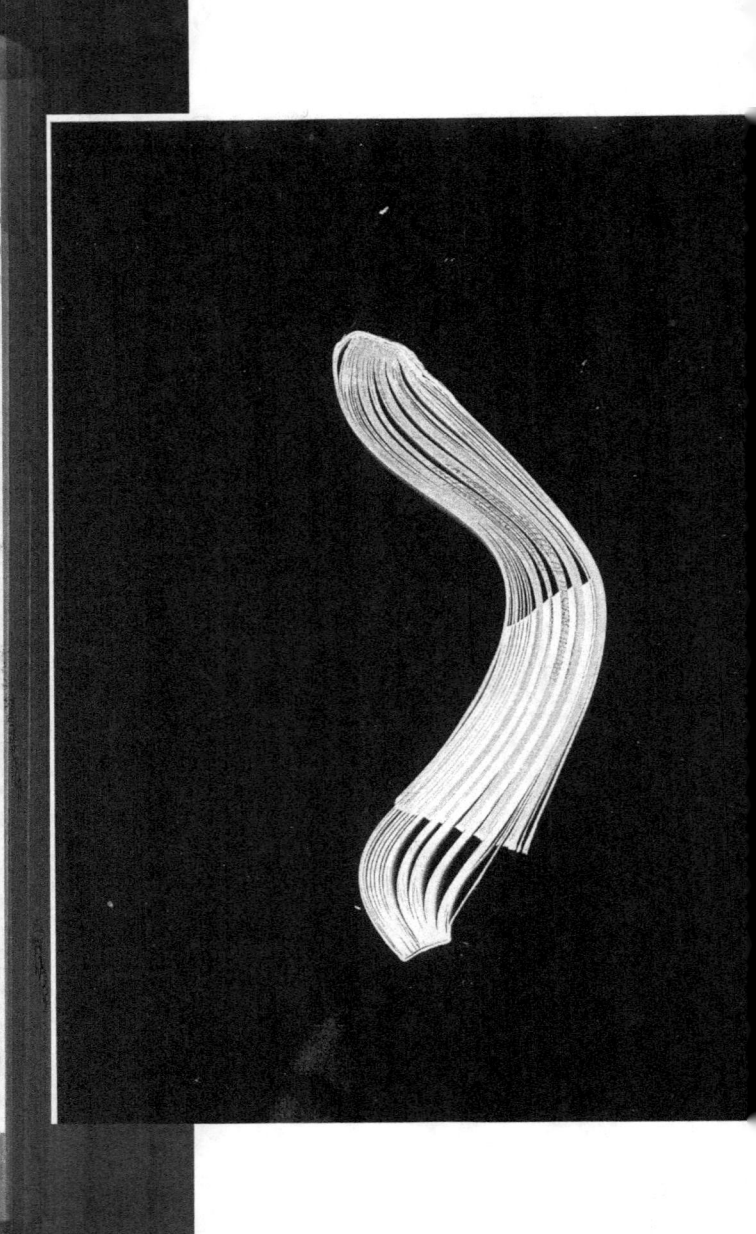

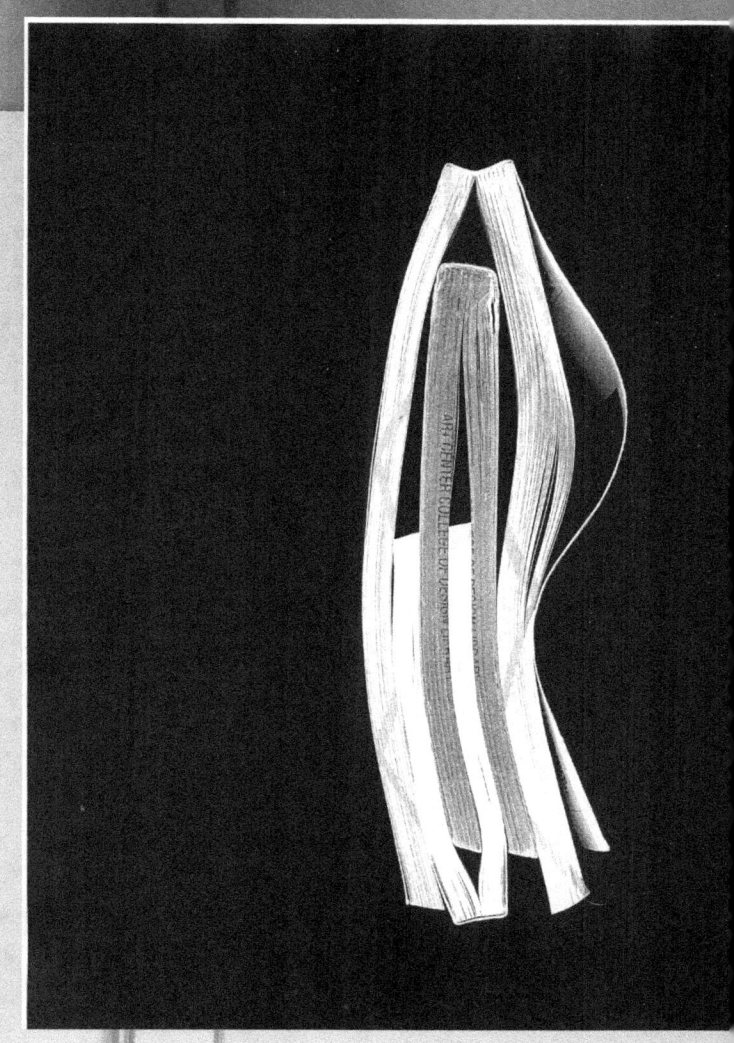

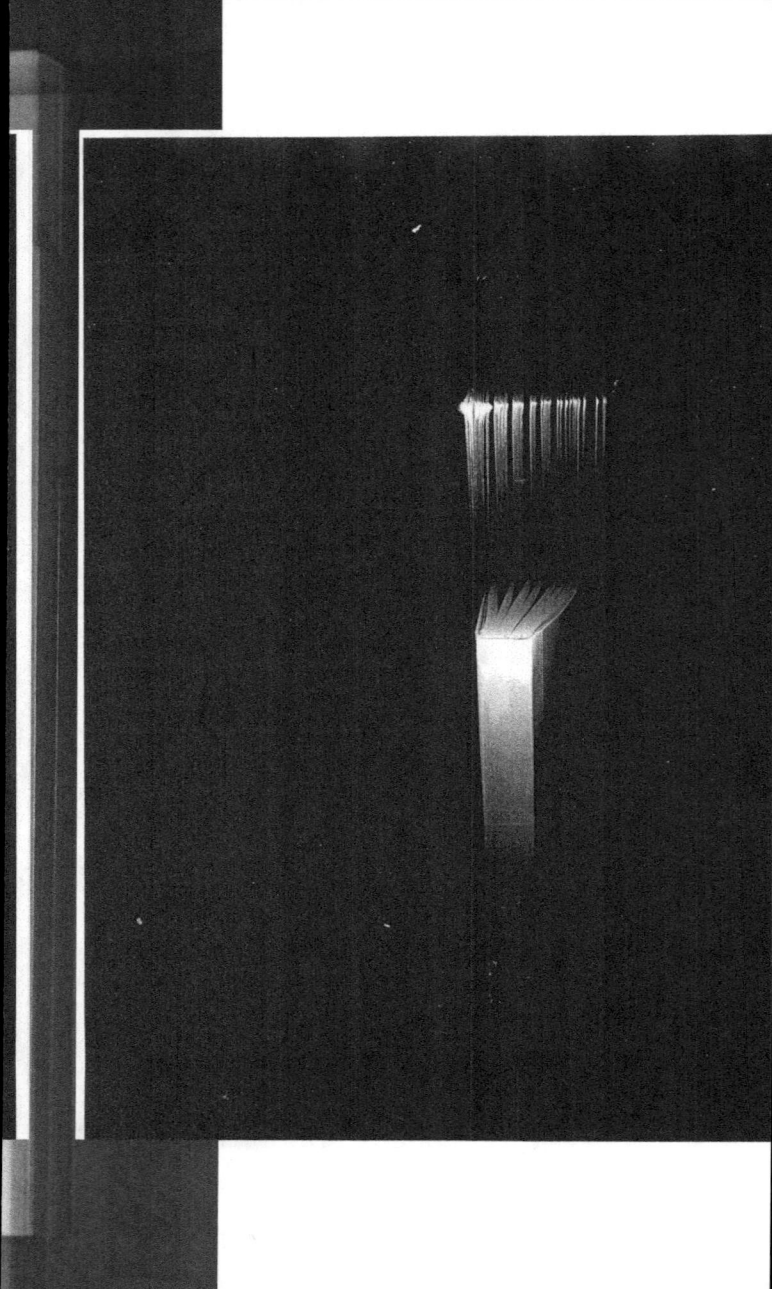

259-0312 KANAGAWA JP

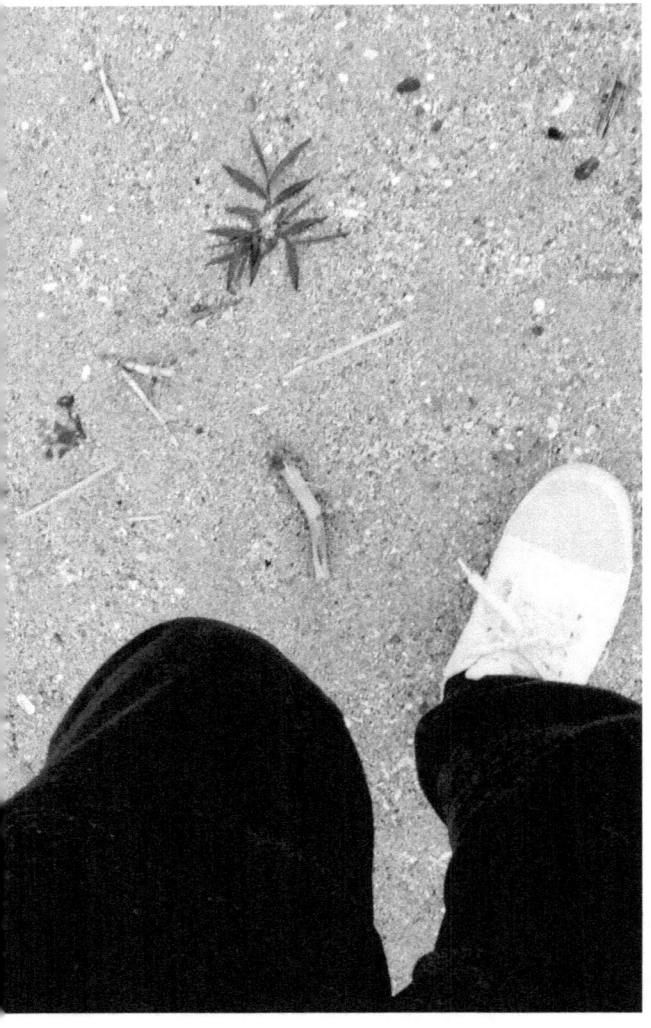

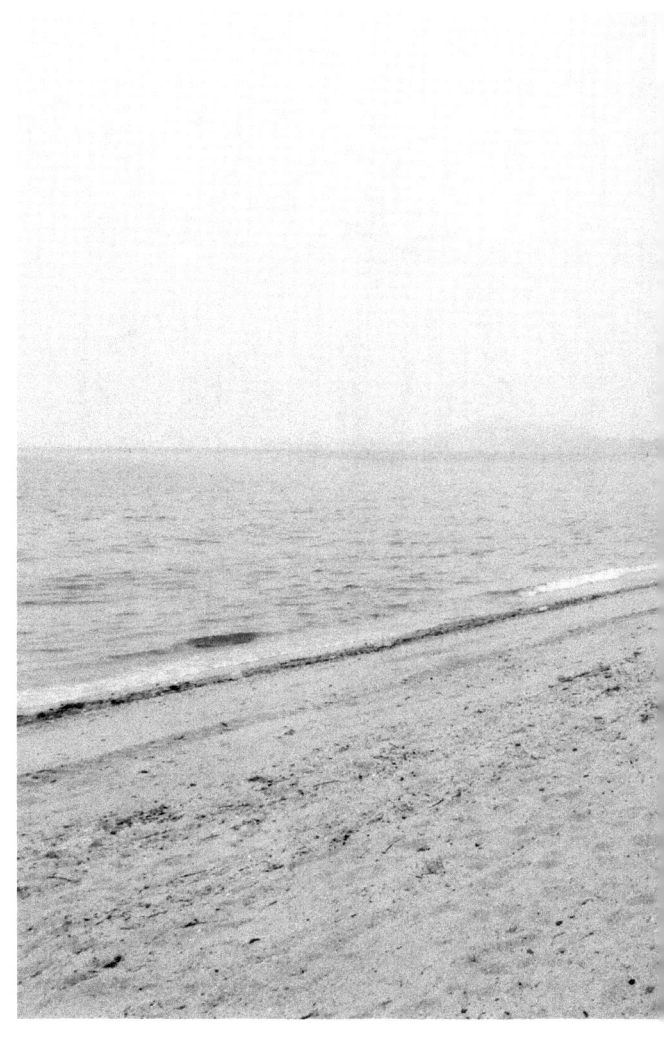

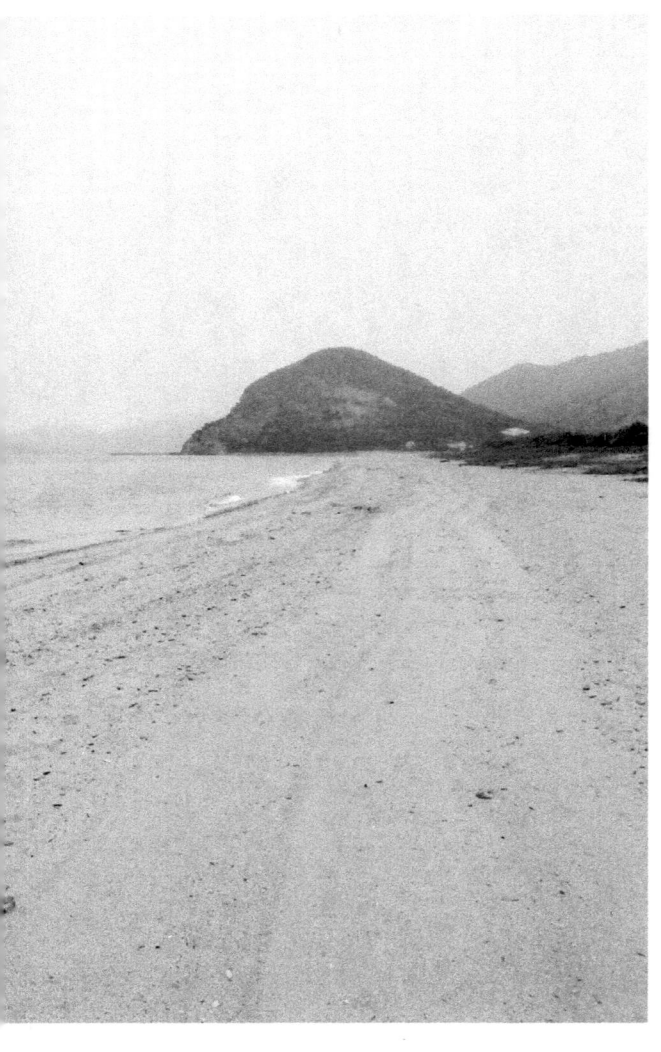

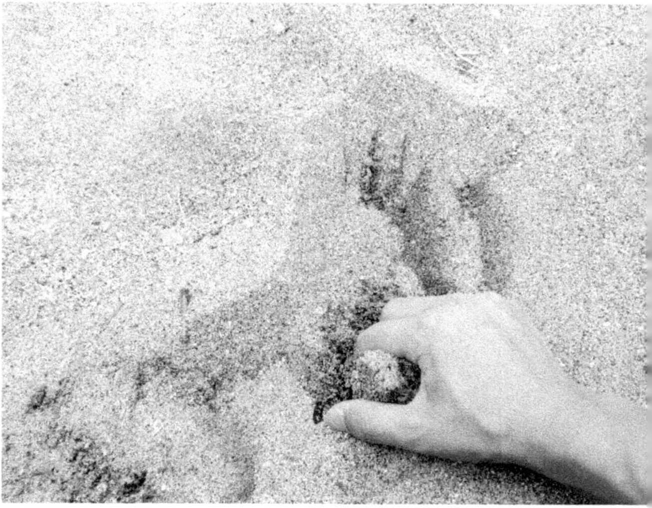

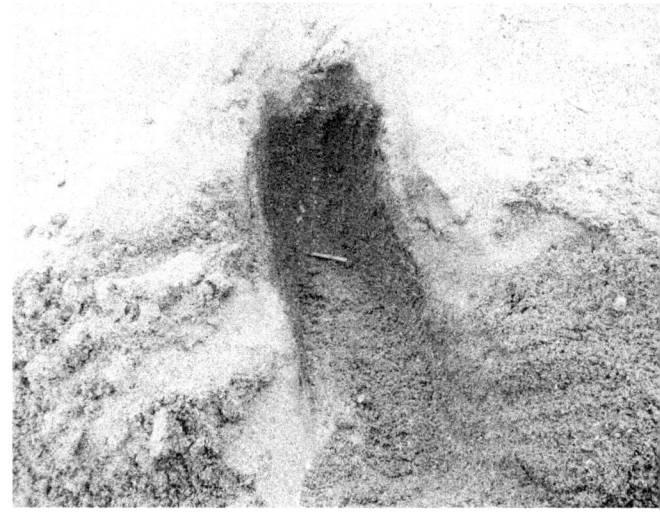

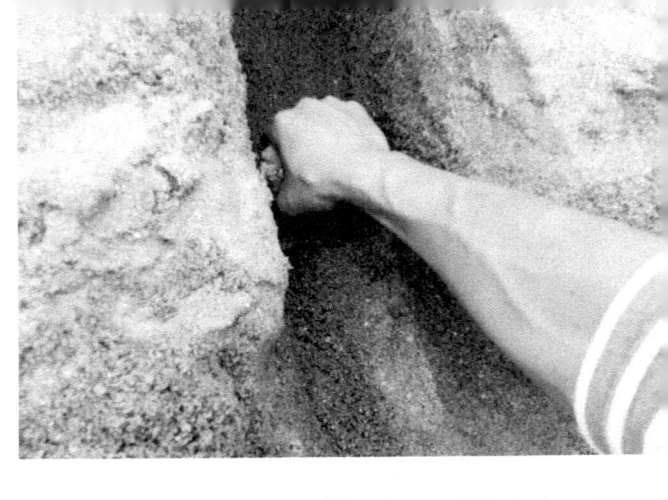

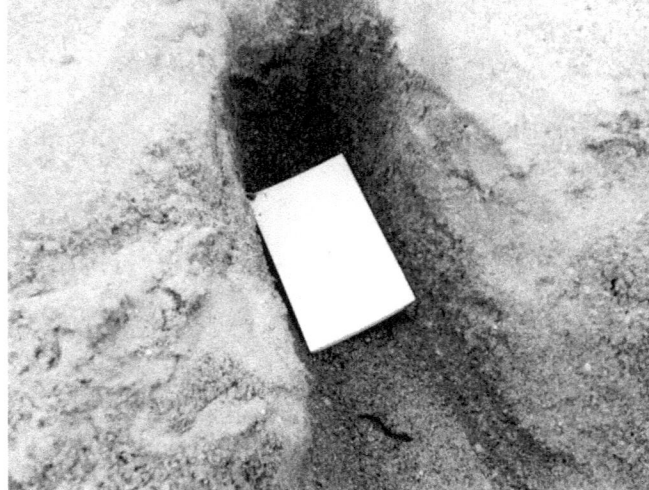

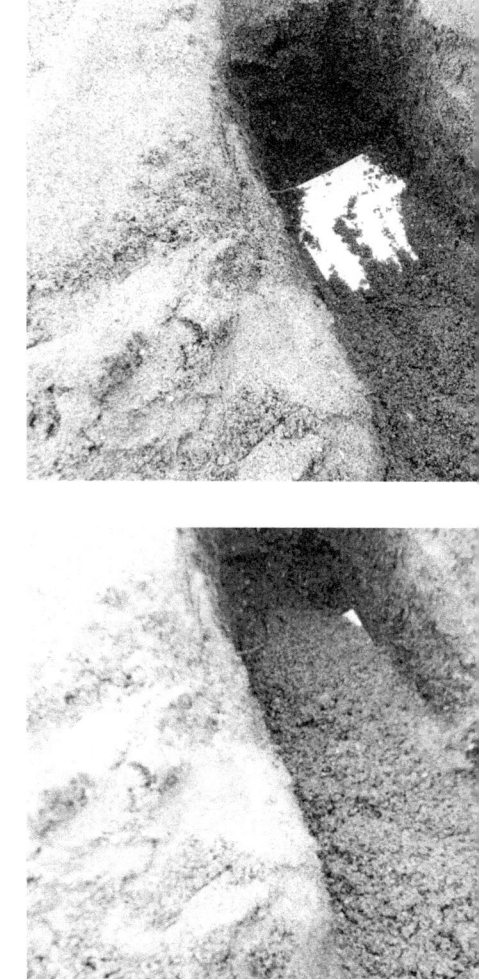

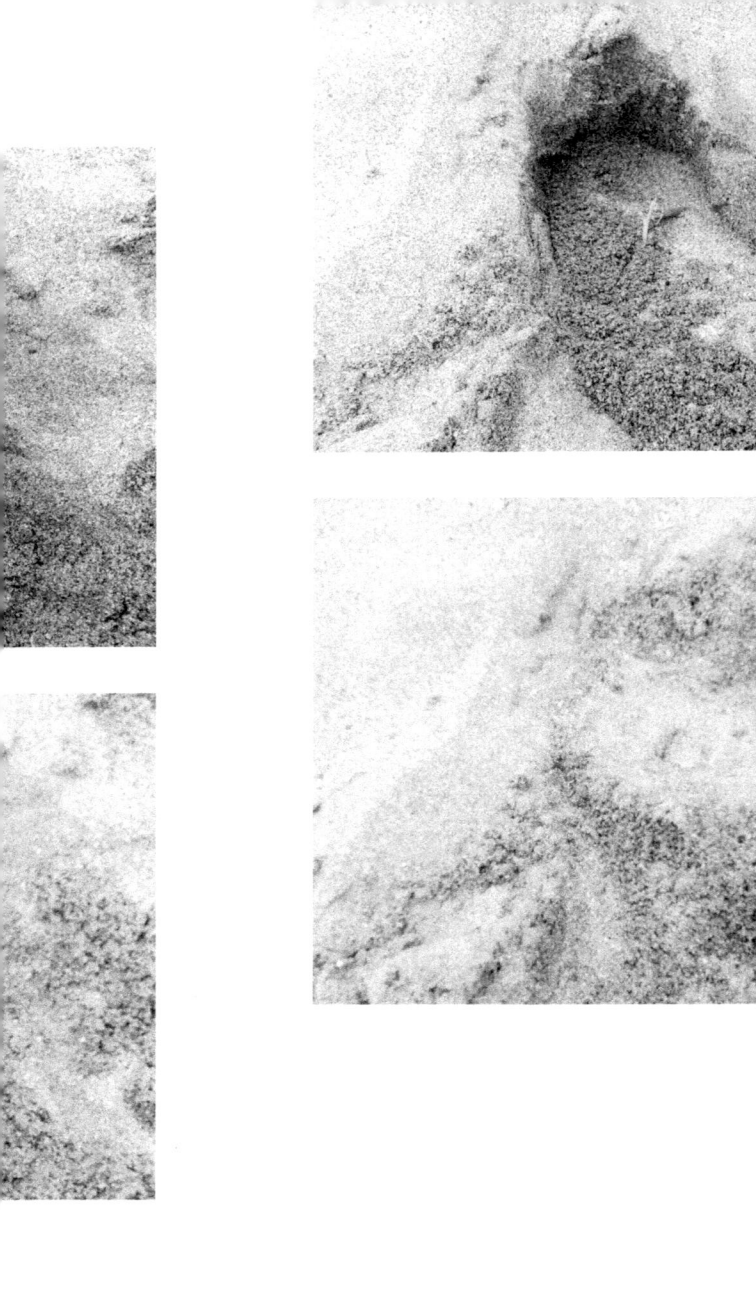

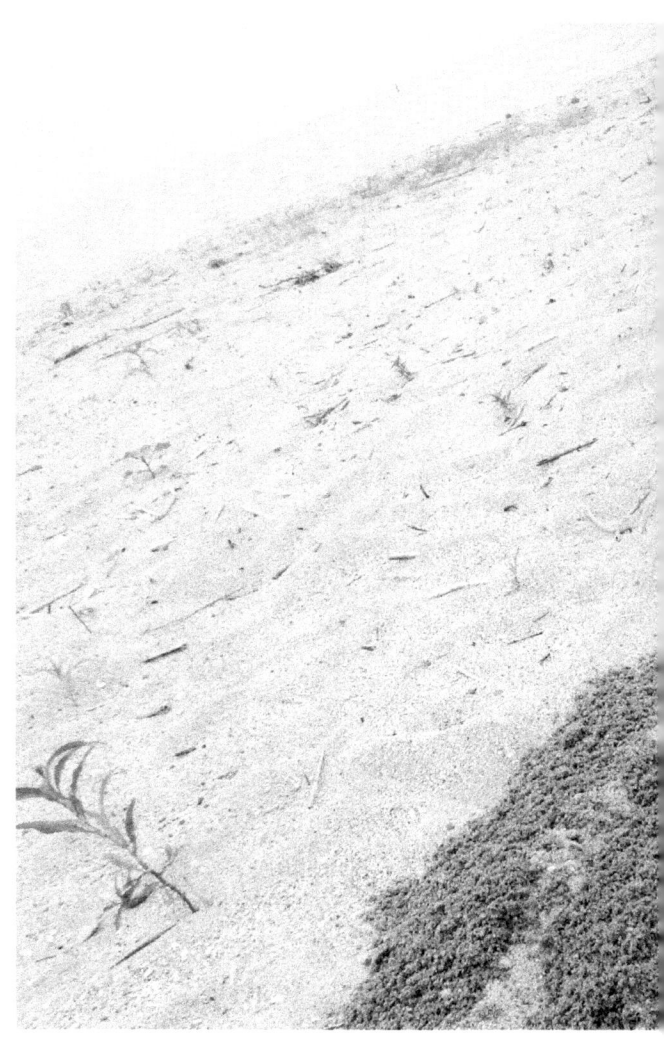

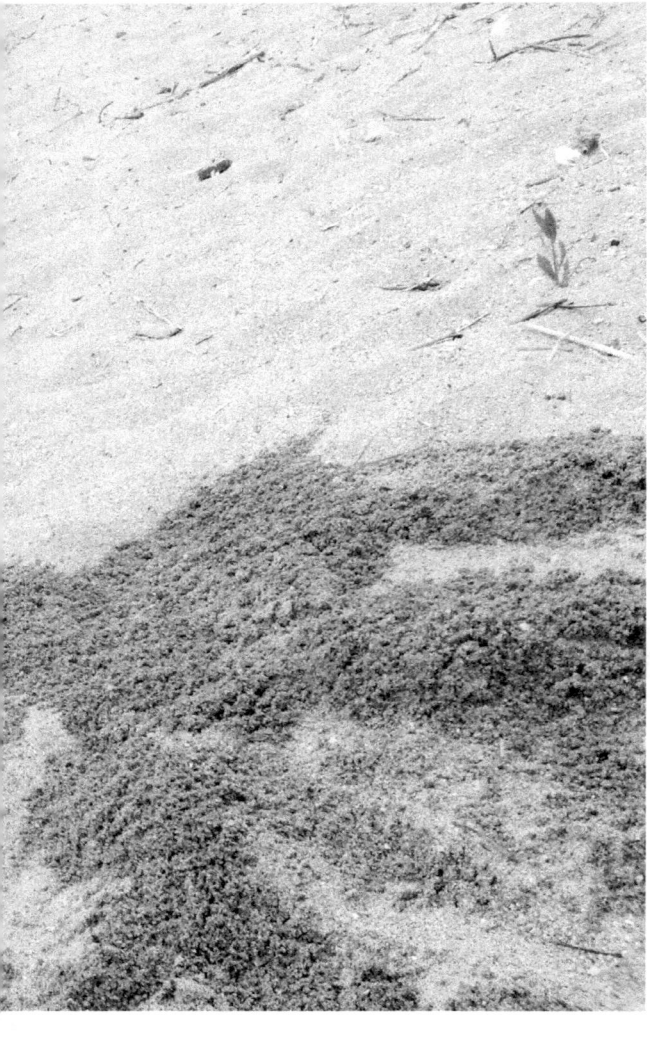

From the vantage point of a graphic designer, documentation has become more than just a way of immortalising a piece of work with photographs. It is no longer just for reference when the need arises, it is no longer just for archiving. In today's context, documentation in itself (more often than not) is – the work. In the digital age today, with just a few clicks, a piece of work has more potential to reach large numbers of virtual audiences than reach the hands of audiences in the actual world. Dissemination of the work on the web requires less resources and reaps better results in terms of marketing/promoting oneself. This calls for graphic designers to create more self-initiated and self-published works as a form of creative expression and self-promotion. Graphic designers often self-publish zines/publications in low quantity or just a single copy, without a client and in turn, without a budget (this is compensated with no client restraints). The design of the work is directly influenced by how it will be documented and disseminated digitally on online portfolios and social media. The image of a publication cover (or a few selected pages) has become more important than the design and content of the inside pages as this is what online audiences want to see to decide whether to comment on the work, add to their moodboards, or place an order. The work is then made to order. A digitized version of a book can hold more significance than the actual physical book in this way.

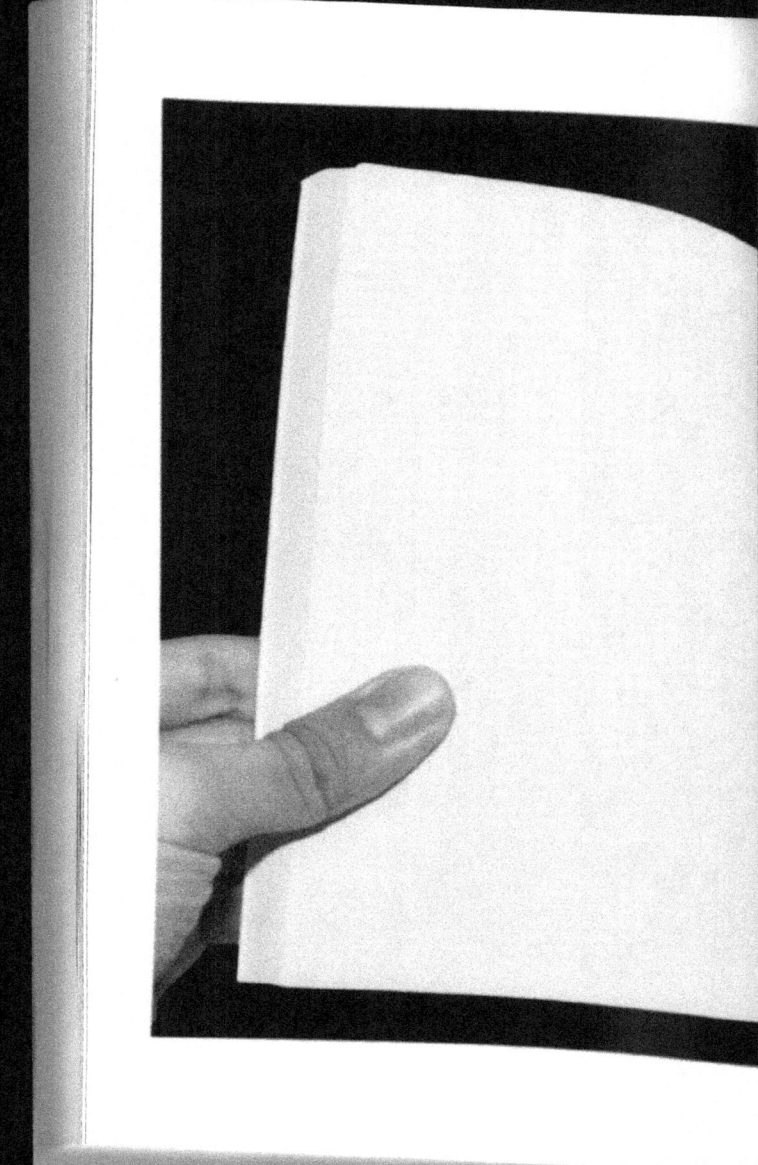

288

CREDITS

7–8
Yvan Martinez,
Joshua Trees,
Krister Olsson

9–21
Federico Antonini

23
Leave the light on,
John Freeman

26–31
What time is this book?,
Joseph Townshend

32–37
Kristian Henson

38–43
*Shower book (14–29 VI
2015)*, Niko Mihaljevic

44–47
Per Törnberg
Image: Sunrise Books

48–53
Lena Wurz

54–55
Luana Graciano

56–61
Seiko Watanabe

63
Simon Goode and
Ira Yonemura

66
Esa Matinvesi

68–69
Hirofumi Isoya

71
Spassky Fischer
(Julia Andreone, Hugo
Anglade, Thomas Petit,
Thomas Petitjean and
Antoine Stevenot)

72–75
Hyunho Choi

77–83
*The Black, Yellow,
Magenta, Cyan, Red,
Green, Blue, Azure,
Beige, Bisque, Brown,
Coral, Cornsilk, Khaki,
Orange, Orchid, Salmon,
Violet, Pink, Firebrick,
Gray, Honeydew, Ivory,
Lavender, Linen, Maroon,
Purple, Mint, Rose,*

Moccasin, Pale, Plum, Sienna, Thistle, Tomato, Turquoise, Violet, Gold, Silver and White Book, Jangs Müller

84–85
Tomoko Kawai

86–87
Cecilia Denti

88–93
Jen Lee

94
Every man's book,
Kevin McCaughey

96–97
The blank book as magnus opus,
Corbin Mahieu

99–101
Jozef Ondrik

102–103
Helge Hjorth Bentsen

104–107
Makoto Yamada

108–119
Sean Kuhnke

120–123
Pimeriko

124–125
GaEun Ryu

127–133
Joana Chicau

136–139
Contemplating Sontag,
Ayse Koklu

140–149
Clara Lobregat Balaguer

150–165
Kasper Pyndt

167
The eraser,
Matheus de Paula

168–170
Marie Lécrivain

172–178: *G.D.A.A*,
site-specific manifesto
and Booq typeface,
Masaki Miwa

179
Booq Alt typeface,
Ying Tong Tan

180–183
Rita Matos

185–223
Luigi Amato

226
Eric Hu

228–231
Ghazaal Vojdani

232
Jan Novák

234–235
Self-publishing,
Neil Donnelly

237
Nobuo Yoda

238–239
Soji Shimizu
Photo: Yusuke Sunaga

242–245
Thomas Hervé

246–249
Re-automata,
Ying Tong Tan

250–255
*Everybody's book of
acting charades
(1897–2015)*,
Claude Marzotto

257–261
David Horvitz

263
Rafaela Drazic

264–265
Risa Tsunegi

266–273
River Jukes-Hudson

274–283
34.136120, 133.640876,
Ryo Shimizu

284–287
Darius Ou Dahao

I0473610